GOD IS *Faithful*

GOD IS Faithful

COMPILED BY
J. B. NICHOLSON JR.

GOSPEL FOLIO PRESS
304 Killaly St. West, Port Colborne, ON L3K 6A6
Available in the UK from JOHN RITCHIE LTD.
40 Beansburn, Kilmarnock, Scotland

GOD IS FAITHFUL
Copyright © 2002
J. B. Nicholson
All rights reserved

Published by Gospel Folio Press
304 Killaly Street West
Port Colborne, ON L3K 6A6

ISBN 1-882701-89-5

ORDERING INFORMATION:
Gospel Folio Press
Phone: 1-800-952-2382
E-mail: orders@gospelfolio.com

Printed in the United States of America

CONTENTS

1. Jehovah Jireh *Wallace & Ruth Logan* 9
2. God of the Impossible *Arthur Gook* 21
3. No Visible Means of Support *David Croudace* 35
4. A Million Answers to Prayer *George Müller* 41
5. Guiding, Providing, Abiding *W. P. W. McVey* 49
6. Reaping What Was Sewn *Pearl Winterburn* 59
7. When God Supplies a "Starving" *H. A. Ironside* 63
8. Two Dimes…and the Lord *R. E. Harlow* 67
9. God Looks after His Business *George Campbell* 71
10. We've Come to Give *R. C. Allison* 75
11. The Burning Issue *Ian Rathie* 81
12. Taking the Test *T. D. W. Muir* 87
13. The Just Shall Live by Faith *Marian Carter* 95
14. Escape! *Conrad Baehr* 105
15. Our Daily Bread *Christopher Willis* 115
16. Step by Step *Charles Stanley* 127
17. Provider and Protector *Abigail Luffe* 133
18. All Along the Way *Andrew Stenhouse*… 153
19. Hitchhiking on Purpose *George Watmough* 169

v

GOD IS FAITHFUL

20. God is in the Details *J. H. Brown* 179
21. How Good is the God We Adore *T. E. Wilson* 187
22. Captured by the N. Vietnamese *Sam Mattix* 205
23. Great is Thy Faithfulness *Gordon Wakefield* 213
24. God Will Take Care of You *George Wiseman* 221
25. When the Circus Comes to Town *John W. Bramhall* 227
26. An Engine in the Wilderness? *David Long* 231
27. God Always Has Someone *Madge Beckon* 239
28. He Will Do It *Joyce Finch* 247
29. The Farm and the School *Della Letkeman* 255
30. God Chooses His Servants *Ransome W. Cooper* 263

PREFACE

It is the desire and intention of the compiler of this collection that the title of the book would be the focus of our hearts. We take as the theme of this little book the words and sentiment of Psalm 115:1,

> *Not unto us, O Lord, not unto us, but unto Thy name give glory, for Thy mercy, and for Thy truth's sake.*

One brief response we received to our request for testimonials to the Lord's faithfulness was sent by Mr. John Bramhall, then in his hundredth year. He wrote:

> I surely can witness to the faithfulness of God through the 70 or more years I have spent in the Lord's work. The truth of Philippians 4:19, *"But my God shall supply all your need according to His riches in glory by Christ Jesus"* has certainly been proved over and over again in our lives, to His glory—even during the early years of the Great Depression. One strange experience

GOD IS FAITHFUL

stands out. In 1935, my wife had major surgery, and the doctor told me to be sure she had eggs for breakfast to help her restore her strength. We had such little income in those days we could not afford that. Believe it or not, some neighbor's chicken—which neighbor, I don't know—strayed every morning into our yard, made a nest, and laid a fresh egg each day during her convalescence. I asked no questions *"for conscience sake"* (1 Cor. 10:25) but my wife had a fresh egg every day while recuperating.

Love in Christ, John Bramhall

These stories of the Lord's faithfulness in the lives of His servants are obviously only a small sampling of the ongoing harvest of fruit that is borne *"which cheereth God and man,"* fruit that develops for no other reason than that His people abide in the Vine.

Special thanks to the "servants' servants" of Christian Missions in Many Lands, Inc., who provided both the inspiration and practical help in forwarding this project along. Without them this book would not have happened.

Deo gratias
J. B. NICHOLSON, JR.

ONE

Jehovah Jireh

Wallace and Ruth Logan were commended from the USA in 1923 to serve the Lord at Chavuma, Zambia. Their family has been a tremendous encouragement to the work of God in Africa. Their children include: Mrs. Viola Young, Mrs. Esther Howell, Mrs. Francis Iler, Mrs. Eleanor Sims, Mrs. Grace Croudace and their two sons, Paul and David who co-authored this chapter.

"All dollar dealings suspended." The telegram was clear and it was enough to strike a cold, gnawing fear into any heart. The year was 1929, the time of the stock market crash. Six years before, Wallace and Ruth Logan had left their family and friends and also a thriving electrical contracting business in Buffalo, NY, to serve the Lord in a remote part of central Africa then known as Northern Rhodesia (now Zambia). They had gone out without the promise of a penny from any individual or organization, looking to God alone to supply their needs.

God had given them a family of three children and He had blessed their efforts among the Africans. Many had trusted Christ as Saviour.

To meet the needs of a growing mission station, they had an extensive building program underway, including the construction of a church building to seat 2000 people. Hired African workers would need payment at the end of the month.

Now they held a telegram from their bank in Africa informing them that because of the unsound dollar, American money would no longer be honored. At that time all their financial support came from the United States and Canada. Not knowing how He would supply, they clung to God in faith trusting His promise in Hebrews 13:5, *"I will never leave thee, nor forsake thee."*

Before the end of the month, when the workmen's payroll was due, there came a check from a Christian they had never heard of in Ireland. The next month there was a gift from New Zealand, then Australia. And so it continued until the American financial crisis had sufficiently resolved so that banks in Africa would once again accept United States currency. Then, interestingly, the other sources quietly dried up.

After that experience Mr. Logan would say, "Even if you quote Hebrews 13:5 backwards, it still holds true, 'Thee forsake, nor thee leave never will I.'"

JEHOVAH JIREH

CANADIAN MILK DELIVERY—IN AFRICA!

"Before they call, I will answer; and while they are yet speaking, I will hear" (Isa. 65:24).

Their home base was Chavuma Mission but they would make evangelistic forays on foot to outlying areas. One such extended trip was planned in the land lying to the west of the Zambezi River. In that remote region no fresh milk was available for their twin toddlers. The obvious answer was to take along powdered milk, but they had none and the nearest store was a 12-week round trip journey by river. Mr. and Mrs. Logan prayed, asking God to provide for the twins.

At that time, the mail came by runner approximately every six weeks from the distant outpost of Broken Hill. The actual arrival, though, varied a great deal. The day before the long trek was to begin the runner arrived and in the mail bag was a package from a Christian woman in Canada. An accompanying note read, "Dear brother and sister Logan, I was downtown shopping buying milk for my baby when I thought of your twins and wondered if you might be glad of some too. I was planning on mailing it another day, but as I passed by a post office right in the store, the Lord seemed to say, 'Why not mail it now?' So I went right to the PO counter and mailed you the can of milk. I hope you receive it all right." It was enough to last the whole time that they would be gone!

GOD IS FAITHFUL

Long before the need had arisen, the Lord had laid it on the heart of this woman to buy and send the powdered milk so that even with the slow mail traveling by boat, train, truck and finally for many miles on foot, it would arrive at exactly the right moment. The Lord even led her when to mail it. If she had purchased the milk, taken it home to wrap it, then mailed it at the usual post office a few days later, it would likely have arrived too late. The timing of the Lord is perfect.

THE LORD'S SPARE PARTS DEPARTMENT

"My God shall supply all your need according to His riches in glory by Christ Jesus" (Phil. 4:19).

There were no schools in that part of Africa in those early days. As their children grew, the problem arose regarding their education. The Lord answered this need for them and for many other missionaries through the opening of the Sakeji School which had two long terms a year. Of necessity, this had to be a boarding school. The 1200 mile round trip was taken four times yearly over rough dirt roads.

On one occasion, the Logans were making this journey in their pickup truck. Being hundreds of miles from the nearest town, Mr. Logan would carry spare truck parts for things that were liable to break down. On this particular trip the vehicle sputtered and came to a stop. In the hot

JEHOVAH JIREH

African sun he raised the hood and, as persistent honey flies buzzed around his head, he checked things out. He found that the fuel pump had chosen that moment to end its useful life. No problem, he had a spare one. When he tried to install it, however, there was no way it would fit. He had been sold the wrong size.

Now what should he do? They were many miles from help on this remote African road. His young family was vulnerable. How would God provide here? The insects continued to buzz…but what was that other sound? Some of the children put their ears to the ground, African fashion, then excitedly said, "A car's coming!" Yes, now there was the distinct hum of an approaching vehicle. As it pulled up they recognized the driver, an agnostic acquaintance. "What's the problem?"

"My fuel pump has broken and the spare one that I have is the wrong size," Mr. Logan replied.

"I have a spare pump," responded the acquaintance, "but I'm afraid it won't fit your truck since my vehicle is a different make and model. By the way, you should make sure you have the right part before you get out into the middle of nowhere!"

"You're right," said Mr. Logan, "but I know the Lord will provide for us."

Unable to be of assistance, the man drove off. But shortly he was back. "In the outside chance that my fuel

GOD IS FAITHFUL

pump might just happen to fit your GMC pickup," he suggested, "let me just check it." He got it out and found to his astonishment that it was the wrong pump for his own vehicle, but exactly the right one for the Logan's truck! "I wish I had a bit of Logan's luck," he exclaimed.

Mr. Logan replied, "You do not need 'Logan's luck,' but what you do need is Logan's God."

Soon the pump was installed and the family was on its way again.

A LAKE JUST FOR US

On another occasion they were hundreds of miles from their mission station, stranded in the sizzling African heat. The faithful GMC pickup had come to a stop with a horrible, grinding sound from the wheel bearing. The burnt smell in the air confirmed their fears—they could not move. In this particular section of Africa vehicles seldom traveled and it could be weeks before another might pass by. What was the family going to do?

The gravity of their plight was apparent when they found that the back-up drinking water bag had developed a leak and had lost all of its precious contents. The bag which they had been using through the morning was almost empty. Mrs. Logan wisely rationed out the remaining life-sustaining liquid in teaspoons, but it was not enough. The relentless African sun beat down without

JEHOVAH JIREH

mercy on the forlorn group.

Behind them lay many miles where there had been no rivers. Before them the distance to the nearest river was unknown. Running out of drinking water is not a pleasant experience. One's mind thinks of similar instances. An elder from the assembly back at the mission station at Chavuma went on a trip, lost his way on a vast African plain, and ran out of water. Search parties found him on the third day close to death. It was said that his tongue had swelled up so much that he could not speak.

As Mr. Logan was dismantling the burnt wheel bearing which had turned blue with heat, somber faces of the little children reflected their serious plight. "Mother," said Paul, "are you sure there's no more water?" The words tugged at the heart of the courageous missionary. Mother Logan was a godly woman who knew how to rise above trials. She had taught her children to look up instead of around. In an effort to cheer up the children, she got them singing choruses. However, this became a problem with their dry throats. The next thing she did was to put into practice the Scriptures, *"Cast your burden upon the Lord and He will sustain you."* She gathered the children around in a circle and each one prayed. What a never-to-be-forgotten prayer meeting! The earnestness of that prayer group of young and old in the burning sun left an indelible impression on the lives of the missionary kids.

What a heritage she was passing on to her children! Although the wording of each prayer differed, the theme was the same, "Lord, we are desperate, please direct us to where we can find water and another wheel bearing." This was one prayer meeting where no one stayed home to do homework.

After prayer the group looked up the road and were delighted to see a bicyclist approaching. The children clapped their hands gleefully. "Look! The Lord has answered our prayer!" The cyclist was asked if there were any rivers in the direction from which he had come. His reply brought a dejected silence, "No, there are no rivers around here." The disappointment written in their eyes was agonizing. What does one do when one prays and the heavens appear to be still, silently mocking?

But this was a good opportunity for this missionary couple to demonstrate to their children in a practical way that God wants us to *"Continue in prayer, and watch in the same with thanksgiving."* Back to prayer they went. There was no flowery wording; no words to impress others. Hearts earnestly besought God's help in this desperate situation. In fact, it seemed that they almost forgot the presence of the others and each one sensed the closeness of the Lord.

The quietness was abruptly interrupted with a shot. "Look up ahead! Can you see what I see?" In the distance a traveler was walking toward them. The obvious question went through each of their minds, "If there are no nearby rivers, how and where would this pedestrian find water for his journey?" The group of stranded travelers, who had earnestly prayed, could hardly wait. The man confirmed that there were no rivers nearby. However, the next bit of news electrified the hearts of all. He went on to say that a short distance ahead, but off the road in the forest, was a lake where hunters were camping. He was willing to lead the missionary family there.

Coming out to that hunter's camp on the lake side was the most beautiful sight in the world! The hunters gave them drinking water, took them in their truck to their destination, and then took a long journey out of their way to obtain a replacement bearing.

Regardless of the trials that God entrusts to His people, He does not forget those who live by faith. *"He that cometh to God must believe that He is and that He is a rewarder of them that diligently seek Him"* (Heb. 11:6).

THE IDEAL TRAVEL AGENT

In 1951, there were nine in the Logan family and it was time for furlough. The chapel at Chavuma Mission had needed major repairs and, as much as possible, all available funds had been poured into these renovations. It was the firm conviction of Wallace and Ruth Logan to neither ask for money nor to make financial needs known to anyone except God alone. They took Him at His Word in Philippians 4:6, *"Let your requests be made known unto God."* They believed that changing the word "God" to "man" would deprive them of the joy of seeing God answer in His own special way.

Enough funds were available for the family to drive 500 miles to the nearest train station and to take the train another 2,500 miles to the port city of Capetown. While in South Africa, God provided the wherewithal to take the ship to Southampton, England. Again while there the needed money, with little left over, was supplied to get the family to the United States.

The ship docked in New York and the family was delighted to be met by some believers in Christ who through the years had been praying for the Lord's work in central Africa. When the luggage was reclaimed on the dock, there was a fee of twenty-four dollars and a few cents. Mr. Logan looked in his wallet. There were four dollars and some change, but that was it. Wondering what to do next, he sighed and rested his hands in his coat pockets. He felt a piece of paper and recalled that one of the Christians who had met them had handed it to him. Pulling it out, he found it was a twenty dollar bill. Handing the money to the official, he said, "There's your twenty-four dollars and twenty-two cents."

JEHOVAH JIREH

It was not long afterward that the Lord very wonderfully provided a new nine-passenger, six-door De Soto sedan in which the whole family could travel while on furlough.

God is great enough for the biggest of needs. But He can also handle the smallest detail. *"There hath not failed one word of all His good promises"* (1 Ki. 8:56).

—Compiled by Paul and David Logan

TWO

God of the Impossible

Arthur Gook, commended from assemblies in England, went to Iceland in 1905, having as his maxim, "Ask God for everything and lack for nothing." By horseback, motorcycle and car, he traversed the country distributing tracts, holding house meetings and talking about the Lord wherever he went.

Eirik was an Icelandic fisherman who lived just outside the village of Hofsos, in the last of a row of fisherman's huts on the rugged cliff overlooking the rough, swelling waters of the mighty Skagafjord—one of the broadest fjords on the north coast of Iceland.

A SUICIDE FRUSTRATED

Poverty had always been one of his nearest acquaintances. Once, faint and hungry through lack of food, Eirik attempted to put an end to his existence, as many other Icelanders have done. He took down his shotgun, loaded it, kicked off his shoe and put the barrel of the gun into his mouth. While fumbling for the trigger with his toe, he passed out and fell. When he revived, he called on God that if there really was a merciful God in the heavens, to give him some food, and prayed that He would send a bird that way for him to shoot. He went down to the beach and looked around. A large bird, of an edible type, came flying past, and with an effort the emaciated man raised his gun and fired. The bird fell, and Eirik thus had his first intimation that God answers prayer.

SAVED TO SERVE

Years passed, and Eirik's long struggle with poverty continued. Motorboats were multiplying and getting the pick of the fishing harvest, and it became increasingly difficult for the owners of small rowing boats, such as Eirik, to pay their way. The long, weary toil on the icy waters of the fjord took a heavy toll of Eirik's health and strength, badly clothed and fed as he was. One day, after great exertion, he hemorrhaged from his lungs. He grew worse and worse, until he had to go to the nearest doctor. He was told there was no cure. He tried another doctor a long way off, with the same result. At last he borrowed money and journeyed to Akureyri, where there were, at the time, three native doctors. He went from one to the

GOD OF THE IMPOSSIBLE

other—his purse getting lighter and lighter and his heart heavier and heavier in the process—and finally was brought to the conclusion that he was incurable. Utter ruin stared him in the face. While in this state of mind, the suggestion was made to him: "Why don't you try the English missionary? It won't cost you anything!"

So he came. I remember the day he walked in to my dispensary and told me that his "back" would bleed. He located the trouble in his back, because that was where he felt the pain. I gave him some medicine, I confess with little hope of success, but with a prayer that it might be helpful to him. He left with some tracts in his pocket, promising to write and let me know how he progressed. A month later, I received a long and enthusiastic letter from him, giving good news of his health, and asking for more medicine. Thus our correspondence began, and before many months had passed, Eirik was able to row his boat with any man, without fearing the distressing recurrence of the hemorrhage.

Best of all, he had found the Saviour of whom I had written to him. His zeal was extraordinary for an Icelander, and he wrote me saying that he longed to use the health God had given him to spread the gospel that had blessed his soul, and he offered to travel round his county and sell Testaments and gospel literature. It seemed fitting to him that the "back" that God had healed should bear a pack of books for God over the hills and valleys of Skagafjord county. He plodded on, week after week, sometimes in deep snow, until practically every house in the county had been visited with the printed message of the gospel.

At first the neighbors could not understand Eirik. Swear words began to be excluded from his vocabulary. The significance of this will be understood when I add that the average Icelander can hardly conduct a simple conversation without continually calling on the Prince of Darkness. Such things showed that Eirik was changed. This caused a sullen, disagreeable opposition to arise.

A MEAN TRICK

One day, after a long spell without any success fishing, the welcome news flew round the village that the fjord was teeming with codfish. There was, however, one important drawback—they had no bait to catch them with. Small pieces of herring were generally used on the Skagafjord fisherman's hooks, but they had caught no herring for several weeks and therefore had no bait. The situation was most tantalizing, especially as the need was so great.

News came, however, by telephone that a trawler had put in at Siglufjord, the next large port along the coast, with a haul of herrings. Hastily the men put their money together and hired a motorboat to send to Siglufjord. Each gave his order for herrings according to his donation. Eirik did not put in an appearance, and the fishermen took the opportunity to play him a mean trick. "We won't let him know anything about herring until it is too late," they said, "and then we'll see how he gets along." The little harbor could not be seen from Eirik's cottage, so it was an easy matter to keep him in the dark.

WHO PILOTED THE HERRINGS?
When the motorboat came back, all the men got busy with their hooks and lines, except Eirik; none would lend or sell him a single herring. Thinking of his wife and four children at home, and their dire need, he made his way up the steep cliff-path with a heart as heavy as lead. It seemed as if God had forgotten him. Before he arrived home, however, the Lord reminded him of one of His promises, and his faith revived. He went into his little hut and cast his burden on the Lord.

Now these hardy toilers of the deep can tell what kind of fish is under the surface of the sea, where a landsman can see no indication of any fish at all. These men of Skagafjord had every reason to believe, according to their knowledge and experience, that herrings had not been in the fjord for weeks, and they did not even think it worthwhile to examine their herring nets. But it occurred

GOD IS FAITHFUL

to Eirik that possibly there might be a few stray herrings in his old patched-up net; in any case it was worthwhile looking, as he had nothing else to do.

I suppose that the men who accompanied Eirik went to see fair play, as they themselves would have been quite equal to annexing the contents of a neighbor's net, and they judged Eirik by their own standard. It was good that they accompanied him. One net after another was drawn up empty, only to be thrown back in disgust, until they came to Eirik's. There seemed to be a hitch somewhere, but at last it came up, full of herrings! Hurriedly drawing up those remaining, they found that there was not a single herring in any of the other nets!

The men were speechless with astonishment, while Eirik praised God for His faithfulness. He had got his herrings for nothing, while the others had paid the full price for theirs at Siglufjord, besides sharing the expense of hiring a motorboat.

I know many of those men. I have sat in their homes and talked to them. Moreover, an account of this event was printed in the Icelandic monthly gospel periodical, Nordurijosid, which, thanks to Eirik's efforts, circulates widely among these fishermen; but I have never heard a word from any of them indicating doubt or criticism of my account of the above event.

The only explanation I can offer is that God caused the

herrings to go in and out around the other nets into Eirik's, to supply the need that he had made known to God, just as Peter experienced as recorded in Luke 5:4-7.

OVERCOMING EVIL WITH GOOD

The last part of this incident is, however, the best. Few would have judged Eirik harshly if he had sold some of his herrings for the same price as they cost at Siglufjord. But God gave him an opportunity to let his light shine for Christ, and he made use of it. Going to those who, by reason of poverty, had not been able to order sufficient herring from Siglufjord for bait, he gave them freely, in spite of their shabby treatment of him only a short time before.

Needless to say, a splendid catch of codfish gladdened the homes of Hofsos that day, but in none was there such joy as in Eirik's little hut.

Is it to be wondered at that Eirik was a successful salesman of gospel literature? Is it to be wondered at that, when Eirik's friend, the missionary, came to Hofsos, the largest building would not hold the crowds that came to hear the gospel preached?

Eirik is now with the Lord, who had done so much for him. On his deathbed, he said to his wife: "Write and tell Mr. Gook that I died with the Name of Jesus on my lips. His life has not been in vain."

Arthur Gook, "Can We Trust Our God?" Sept.-Nov. 94 *Counsel*, pp.4-5

COAL FROM HEAVEN

Perhaps the most remarkable proof, within my personal experience, of the watchful interest shown by our heavenly Father in the details of His children's lives, is furnished by an incident which took place in Iceland early in the days of the First World War.

The German submarine campaign had disorganized shipping between Britain and Iceland. Of the few ships which sailed regularly between the two countries, several had been either mined or sunk by submarines. It became exceedingly difficult for Iceland to obtain sufficient supplies of coal for the winter. The little that was available at Akureyri, in the north of Iceland, was quickly sold at a high price.

A SURPRISE MESSAGE

One of our greatest difficulties was in heating the hall for our meetings. My wife and her maid, who met with difficulties at every turn on account of the absence of coal in the household, made special prayer to God that He would be pleased to supply this pressing need. To me it seemed impossible that this request should be granted. No coal was obtainable in the town, nor was there any prospect of supplies coming at that time of the year from Britain. Still, I believed that the Lord would help us in some way or other over our difficulties. But the Lord did

GOD OF THE IMPOSSIBLE

"exceeding abundantly above all" that we asked or thought. *"With God all things are possible"* (Mt. 19:26).

One evening, early in January, when the heating problem was becoming acute, I received a phone call from Reykjavik. It was the French Consul, who informed me that a French vessel had arrived there and had on board five tons of coal for me. He could give me no information as to the shipper, and wanted to know what to do with the coal, as it had to be disposed of at once. Taken by surprise, I was at a loss what instructions to give, but I promised to contact him next morning.

It was a good thing to have five tons of coal, but it could do us little good in Reykjavik, 200 miles away! There was no prospect of a ship leaving for our port, Akureyri, for some months.

I went to see a coal merchant in the town, and he estimated the cost of shipping the coal from Reykjavik to Akureyri, at current freight charges, to be almost twice the worth of the coal! Then he confided in me that there was a quantity of coal already in the town, but it was the property of a man in Reykjavik, who owned several steam trawlers, and who was jealously hoarding it for his boats the following summer, when coal might be more scarce.

"If you could only get him to take your coal, and let you take five tons of his here!" he said, "but I'm afraid it

GOD IS FAITHFUL

will be hopeless, for the Akureyri Town Council begged him to sell them coal for the townspeople, and he refused. He won't let anyone touch his coal."

"Who is looking after the coal for him?" I asked. He mentioned a man I knew very well who was the only other coal merchant in the town.

I went straight to his house and put the matter before him. "I want you to phone the owner of this coal and ask him to exchange five tons of coal with me. He could take my coal from the French ship at Reykjavik, and I would take five tons of his here."

"It's not a bit of good!" replied the merchant, "he has refused the urgent request of the Town Council, and he won't even let me have any of it for my use, although I am his friend and agent."

"Well, we'll try, anyway," I said; "if you don't mind phoning, I will pay for the call."

He got a connection with the man in Reykjavik in a surprisingly short time, but on stating my request, met with an abrupt refusal. The man wanted coal in Akureyri, not in Reykjavik.

But while the merchant was telephoning to Reykjavik, I was telephoning to heaven! My friend changed the subject and spoke on the phone about other business for a short time, then reverted to his original request about my coal. The man at the other end asked who it was that wanted to change the coal. After a moment's hesitation, during which I was calling on God to cause him to give way, the man at the other end said, "Oh, very well, let him have it. Tell him to send me a wire tomorrow authorizing me to take over his coal."

I went home that evening the possessor of five tons of coal, probably the only one so fortunate in the whole of the north of Iceland. On arriving home, I found a cable awaiting me from London, informing me of the shipment, and a parcel. The sender's name was unknown to me.

Shortly after this, reports came in that Greenland ice was invading the north coast of Iceland. It often happens that immense fields of ice are carried away by storm or current from the coasts of Greenland and borne towards the south. The action of the waves causes them to break up, and as they proceed further south they gradually melt. Sometimes these icebergs prove dangerous to ships crossing the Atlantic, as in the case of the *Titanic*.

A "MISTAKE" OVERRULED

I had been living thirteen years in Akureyri, and all that time I had never seen an iceberg. This time, however, I was going to see considerably more of them than I cared for. A tremendous frost heralded the approach of the hoary giants, and before long the whole of the north of Iceland where we lived lay in the grip of this icy invader.

Then it was that we traced the wondrous hand of God in leading the consignors of the coal to despatch it to Reykjavik instead of Akureyri. In ordinary circumstances this would have been the wrong thing. However, the One who knew that thousands of square miles of icebergs were on their way to the north of Iceland, and that a stock of coal in Akureyri could be exchanged, caused the senders to despatch the coal to Reykjavik. If they had waited for a ship going direct to Akureyri, the coal could not have reached us until months later, for the ice blockaded us more effectively even than the German submarines.

"SCIENCE" PUT TO THE PROOF

As we needed food as well as fuel, I thought I would sell some of the coal. The local doctor told me that he was very anxious to buy some coal for the hospital. This was not a charitable institution; every service was charged for, so I did not hesitate to sell the coal at the usual price.

Although the doctor was not a believer in the Lord Jesus, he was always friendly. I told him how God had sent us the coal. He listened with interest and said when I finished: "Oh! that's easily explained on a scientific basis. It's an interesting instance of telepathy. Your prayers caused thought waves; some sensitive person in Britain received an impression from them, and sent you the coal. It was no answer to prayer as you understand it."

A little later I said, "Let me see, doctor, will you not be in great need of coals for the hospital when these you are now buying are exhausted?"

"Yes, indeed," he replied, "I don't know what I shall do if the weather keeps on like this. I'm doing all I can to get coal, but it is impossible."

"Well," I said, "I will tell you how you can get five tons." He listened with intense interest. I continued: "All you have to do is to think about it as hard as you can and send out some very powerful thought waves. Some sensitive person in Britain or elsewhere will receive an impression from you and send the coals. This, according to you, is the way my coals came, and you ought to be able to do as well. We are now in January. I will give you to the end of March to get your coal."

My friend collapsed. I then informed him in very direct language that he knew as well as I did that all the telepathy in the world would never have brought five tons of coal in such unusual circumstances, and that only the wisdom and power of Almighty God, the Creator of heaven and earth, could possibly have answered our feeble cry and supplied our need. I hope he learned his lesson.

EVIDENCE OF DIVINE GUIDANCE

I heard later that God had so burdened the hearts of

some of His children in England with our need of fuel that they, with persistent effort and even personal representations to the Admiralty, were able to obtain permission to send the coal.

The ship decided on was the *Bisp,* a Danish steamer that was to leave for Iceland about that time. For some unknown reason this was changed and the coal was ordered to be sent by the French vessel instead. The *Bisp* ran aground and had to return to dock for inspection and repair. Could human judgment have foreseen this?

Needless to say, this wonderful manifestation of God's care for us greatly strengthened our faith. Every shovelful of coal was a reminder of His faithfulness. Indeed, I may say that it was a blessed lesson to many who knew the circumstances.

Arthur Gook, *Can a Young Man Trust His God?,* London: Pickering & Inglis, n.d., pp. 31-37.

THREE

No Visible Means of Support

David and Grace Croudace were commended as missionaries in 1958 to a part of Zambia, known in those days as "the most remote corner of the British Empire." For over 40 years they have been taking the gospel to the villages and also have been reaching thousands of young people through teaching Bible in Government High Schools. As a result they have seen many N. T. assemblies planted. Fifteen years ago their Bible teaching ministry extended to Malawi and Mozambique where they now spend part of each year.

"You're throwing your life away!" my workmate retorted when I resigned my job as an accountant to follow the Lord's leading to take the gospel to those who had never heard it. "Give up your career? How are you going to support yourself?" an older Christian barked out when I told him of what I believed the Lord wanted me to do.

After spending my savings on further training, I graduated from the Missionary School of Medicine in London, and set out for Lukolwe in Zambia (then N. Rhodesia) to join John and Eleanor Sims in a new outreach. I took with me all that I owned in this world—a tin trunk not much larger than a suitcase, a small second-hand tent, two very old motorbikes, and the equivalent of about $8—all that was left of my savings.

As I bumped along in a local bus for three days, getting covered in red dust, the questions I had been asked when I left my secular work kept coming back to my mind. After all, no one had promised to support me in any way! In fact I had been told by a group of elders, "Don't look to us for support!"

Thoughts kept coming: I could have still been back in my old office, responsible for administering over £2,000,000 each week. Yet here I was, heading out into the bush with no visible means of support. Was I throwing my life away? Had I made a terrible mistake? But I had heard my Saviour call and, having put my hand to the plow, there could be no going back.

Furthermore, the Word of God graciously assured me that *"my God shall supply all your need according to His riches in glory by Christ Jesus"* (Phil. 4:19). I realized that just as I had put my faith in the Lord Jesus Christ some years before to save me, so now I must quietly go forward with my faith resting only in Him, the One who was sending me, and I must depend on Him alone to provide for every need.

BIG BUMPS IN LIFE

After some months of language study, I joined the Sims in reaching out into the surrounding area. This included a weekly motorbike ride of about 40 miles, on what were only "tracks" through the bush, in order to take the gospel to three schools. It was hot and tiring but thrilling to do the "circuit" each week and see the entire student body of young people crowding into one classroom, drinking in the gospel message—in spite of my faltering Luvale. Some turned to Christ in repentance and faith, and some of those who were saved then, are today elders in assemblies in distant parts of Zambia. Was my life being thrown away?

On the last day of the school term I was riding home, when I hit a rather bigger bump than usual, and my precious motorbike broke right in half! I was shattered! It wasn't the sixteen-mile walk home or the loss of the bike so much as the thought that without transport I would no longer be able to do the rounds of these schools and give the gospel to these young people. The bike was so old that it had metal fatigue and proved to be beyond repair. The devil then reminded me of all the questions he had thrown at me earlier.

GOD IS FAITHFUL

While I had been commended to the work of the Lord by the elders of my assembly, no human being had promised to support me. I could not write to my elders asking them to send me a new bike. I poured out my soul to the Lord as I trekked through the heavy sand along the winding footpath, until I finally arrived back at my little grass roofed house on the station. I was reminded again and again that it was the Lord who had sent me. Yes! Not only had He sent me, but He had also promised to supply my every need. I could give my "report" to Him.

But what about the problems? Were they not too big for the Lord to take care of? After all, the schools would re-open in only three months time! I would need something to use if I was to continue in this outreach! Only three months! How could a new motorbike come to me in this remote corner of Africa in three months? Where would it come from anyway? How could I possibly find money to buy a new motorbike? As these questions and many others filled my mind, the Lord quietly reminded me that while there was nothing I could do about it, I could just simply tell it all to Him. Yes, just tell Him the whole problem and leave it there. He would know what to do. He knew about it anyway, but He delighted to hear one in need pour out his heart to his Lord. Needless to say, I did this many times in the ensuing weeks.

THE ON-TIME GOD

Three months later when the schools opened, I was riding the "circuit" again—on a brand new Triumph Tiger motorbike!

His ways are past finding out. He had had it all planned long before. There was a young missionary needing encouragement to continue living by faith. Far away there was a group of very new believers, whom I had never met, wanting to get involved in being *"workers together with Him."*

Without any requests or "reports" being sent, the Lord simply brought the two together—we met at the throne of grace. They had heard about the work at Lukolwe and in their first love for their Master, with their hearts in tune with Him, I guess He found it very easy to get their attention. Although I did not know them at all, they wrote and asked if I could use a motorbike! Not only that, but they sent it just in time for the school outreach to continue, without our missing a week! So there I was, back in the saddle, going down the same path through the forest, ready to tell the young people once again about the wonderful Saviour. The only difference, instead of the "cry" from my heart, there was now a "song" in my heart. I had learned in a very practical way that it is, indeed, no vain thing to trust the living God.

SAME-DAY SERVICE

More than forty years have passed and Grace and I are able to echo the same song I sang that day, as we see the Lord alive and at work in so many ways in our daily routine. He seems to delight in such "three way" conversations.

One morning, as Grace had her time of quiet with the Lord, she felt led to give a blanket and a dress to a certain very needy sister. So she put them together in a package. To her surprise that very sister came later in the day for a visit. As she opened the package which Grace handed to her and saw what was in it, her face beamed, and raising her eyes to heaven, she burst forth in prayer, "Heavenly Father," she said, "now I know that You really do care for me. It was just this morning I told You about my need of a blanket and a dress, and You have already heard and answered!" We were as thrilled as she was, to be reminded that whether we live by faith, or give by faith, God is very much alive, hearing our prayers, guiding our giving and keeping His promises.

FOUR

A Million Answers to Prayer

Born in Prussia in 1805, George Müller disappointed his father by squandering his early years on reckless living. At the age of twenty, a university friend invited him to a home Bible study, where Müller was saved. In 1835, he opened an orphanage in Bristol. His objective was twofold: he wanted to care for the needy children and he wanted to prove to the world that God will supply anyone's needs who trusts in Him and prays. When he died in 1898, Müller had housed and educated over 10,000 children.

George Müller is best remembered for his orphanages on Ashley Down in Bristol, England where, eventually, they were caring for 2,000 children. He not only prayed down provision for the Orphan Homes but was a major supporter of mission work around the world and Christian literature distribution through the Scriptural Knowledge Institute which he founded two years before commencing the orphanage work. During his lifetime he handled more than £1,500,000 in donations, an astronomical sum in today's money. And all by taking his needs only to the Lord in prayer.

There was an obvious need to care for the many desperately needy children in 19th century England. But George Müller had a vision larger than the immediate need. Here is his own explanation for the desire he had to establish the children's work:

> It may be well to enter somewhat minutely into the reasons which led me to establish an Orphan House. I had constantly cases brought before me, which proved that one of the special things which the children of God needed in our day was to have their faith strengthened. I longed to have something to point to, as a visible proof, that our God and Father is the same faithful God as He ever was; as willing as ever to prove Himself to be the living God, in our day as formerly, to all who put their trust in Him.
> A. J. Rendle Short (compiler), *The Diary of George Müller,* Grand Rapids, MI: Zondervan, 1974, p. 46.

ONE MORE NIGHT MAKES THE DIFFERENCE

Müller had received complaints about the orphans; his early location was on Wilson Street, in a residential area. He felt the home should be moved to a larger property and on February 3, 1846, saw the vacant land at Ashley Down. As confirmation, one sovereign was anonymously

A MILLION ANSWERS TO PRAYER

dropped into the orphan-box with a slip of paper wrapped around it that simply said, "The new Orphan House."

On February 4 and 5, Müller wrote in his diary:

> Feb. 4—This evening I called on the owner of the land on Ashley Down, about which I had heard on the 2nd, but he was not at home. As I, however, had been informed that I should find him at his house of business, I went there, but did not find him there either, as he had just left before. I might have called again at his residence, at a later hour, having been informed by one of the servants that he would be sure to be at home about eight o'clock; but I did not do so, judging that there was the hand of God in my not finding him at either place; and I judged it best therefore not to force the matter, but to "let patience have her perfect work."
>
> Feb. 5—Saw this morning the owner of the land. He told me that he awoke at three o'clock this morning and could not sleep again till five. While he was thus lying awake, his mind was all the time occupied about the piece of land...and he determined that if I should apply for it, he would not only let me have it, but for £120 per acre, instead of £200; the price which he had previously asked for it. How good is the Lord!...
>
> Observe the hand of God in my not finding the owner at home last evening! The Lord meant to speak to His servant first about this matter, during a sleepless night, and to lead him to fully decide, before I had seen him. —A. E. C. Brooks, *Answers to Prayer from George Müller's Narratives*, Chicago: Moody, n.d.

GOD IS FAITHFUL

WHO HOLDS THE WIND IN HIS FIST?

Near the end of November 1857, Mr. Müller was informed of a boiler leak at one of the orphanage buildings. It was impossible to face the winter without heat.

Various options were considered but none thought feasible, except shutting down the boiler fire, taking down the brickwork that housed the machine, and repairing the leak if possible; hopefully the whole boiler would not have to be replaced.

A date was set for the repairs to begin. But, as Müller records the incident:

> ...A bleak north wind set in. It began to blow either on Thursday or Friday before the Wednesday afternoon when the fire was to be let out. Now came the first really cold weather.... What was to be done? The repairs could not be put off. I now asked the Lord for two things, viz., that He would be pleased to change the north wind into a south wind, and that He would give to the workmen "a mind to work"...Well, the memorable day came. The evening before, the bleak north wind blew still; but, on the Wednesday, the south wind blew: exactly as I had prayed. The weather was so mild that no fire was needed.
>
> The brickwork is removed, the leak is found out very soon, the boiler makers begin to repair in good earnest. About half-past eight in the evening, when I was going home, I was informed at the lodge that the acting principal of the firm, whence the boiler makers came, had arrived to see how the work was going on and

whether in any way he could speed the matter. I went immediately therefore, into the cellar...In speaking to the principal of this, he said in their hearing, "The men will work late this evening, and come very early again tomorrow."

"We would rather, Sir," said the leader, "work all night."

...Thus it was: by the morning the repair was accomplished...and all the time the south wind blew so mildly that there was not the least need of a fire. (*Ibid.*, pp. 57-60.)

THE CRYING BABY

Müller went one day to preach in the Free Assembly Hall, Edinburgh, and the place was packed to overflowing. A well-known agnostic, inspired by curiosity, pressed his way into the hall. Just when the preacher began to deliver his address, a young mother attempted to leave the building because her baby began to cry rather loudly, but the crowd was so great that exit was impossible. Mr. Müller came at once to the troubled mother's help by saying, "Will that dear mother sit down, and we shall ask Jesus to put the baby to sleep."

The mother quietly took her seat, and the assembly bowed while Müller prayed: "Blessed Lord Jesus Christ, be pleased to put this baby to sleep." Immediately the child went to sleep, to the evident astonishment of the audience. The agnostic was startled beyond measure and said to himself, "If that man has a God like that, it is time for me to seek Him." Under the power of the Spirit he sought and found Müller's God. He became an earnest advocate of the faith he so long tried to destroy, and God used him to win many souls to Christ.

NO FOGGY THINKING

Charles Inglis, the well-known evangelist, tells the following story of George Müller:

> When I first came to America, thirty-one years ago, I crossed the Atlantic with the captain of a steamer who was one of the most devoted men I ever knew. When we were off the banks of Newfoundland he said to me, "Mr. Inglis, the last time I crossed here, five weeks ago, one of the most extraordinary things happened that has completely revolutionized the whole of my Christian life. Up to that time I was one of your ordinary Christians. We had a man of God on board, George Müller of Bristol. I had been on that bridge for twenty-two hours, and never left it. I was startled by someone tapping me on the shoulder. It was George Müller.
>
> "'Captain,' he said, 'I have come to tell you that I must be in Quebec on Saturday afternoon.' (This was Wednesday).
>
> "'It is impossible,' I said.
>
> "'Very well, if your ship can't take me, but I have never broken an engagement in fifty years.'
>
> "'I would willingly help you. How can I? I am helpless,' said the Captain.
>
> "'Let us go down to the chart room and pray,' said Mr. Müller.

A MILLION ANSWERS TO PRAYER

"I looked at the man and thought to myself, What lunatic asylum could the man have come from? I never heard of such a thing. 'Mr. Müller,' I said, 'do you know how dense the fog is?'

"'No,' he replied, 'my eye is not on the density of the fog, but on the living God who controls every circumstance of my life.' He got down on his knees and prayed one of the most simple prayers.

"I muttered to myself, 'That would suit a children's class where the children were not more than eight years old.'

"The burden of his prayer was something like this: 'O Lord, if it is consistent with Thy will, please remove this fog in five minutes, Thou knowest the engagement Thou didst make for me in Quebec for Saturday. I believe it is Thy will.'

"When he finished I was going to pray, but he put his hand on my shoulder and told me not to pray. 'First, you do not believe He will; and second, I believe He has, and there is not need to pray.'

"And, as George Müller said, the fog had lifted."

A. Naismith, *1200 Notes, Quotes and Anecdotes,* London: Pickering & Inglis, 1963, p. 155.

FIVE

Guiding, Providing, Abiding

Mr. and Mrs. W. P. W. McVey went from Northern Ireland in 1948 to serve the Lord in Malaysia (then called Malaya). They later served in Singapore, Thailand, and in Hong Kong with the Rooftop Schools. They presently make their home in Australia where they continue in the Lord's work.

During 1948 there occurred two historic events of special interest to Bible students, namely, the rebirth of Israel as a nation and the formation of the World Council of Churches. More importantly to me, however, 1948 was also the year in which I stepped into full-time service for the Lord, believing He would both guide and provide in the days ahead. And that is just what He has so faithfully done from then until now.

ONLY A STEP

As the end of 1947 approached and my days with the

Department of Education were coming to an end, I felt sure enough about the Lord's call, but was by no means sure what my next step should be. Where and how would I begin? In that frame of mind I went to our weekly prayer meeting and found a stranger there. It was Leonard Mullan, who was just then preparing to leave for missionary service in Japan. He had come specially to see me, in the hope that I would join him in a gospel effort in his home town before he left. He explained that his sailing date was uncertain—not uncommon in the years following World War II—and he might have to leave at short notice, in which case I could carry on with the meetings alone. And so it turned out. Leonard and I had a few happy weeks together before he left, and we were both greatly encouraged to see souls won for Christ.

For the next two years I had equally happy relations with some older preaching brethren, from whose lives and lips I learned many needful lessons. One such was D. L. Craig, my father in the faith, a man who lived to a ripe old age and prayed for me every day. But I already had a deepening urge to go to the Far East, with the Chinese race specially in mind. Thinking in terms of a life-long commitment, I felt a knowledge of Chinese would be a real asset. So I enquired, and found that the University of London was offering the very course I wanted. This I took to be further confirmation of the

GUIDING, PROVIDING, ABIDING

Lord's leading, and in due course set sail for Malaya (now known as Malaysia).

Shortly before my arrival in Malaya from the British Isles, Miss Betty Dyer had come from the other side of the world (Tasmania, Australia), and she too was engaged in Chinese studies. Later she became my life partner and co-worker in the service of the Lord. We made our first home among a Chinese community in the town of Seremban, after wonderfully finding a house with a covered courtyard, tailor-made for meetings.

"WITH" AND "BEFORE"

In Seremban we soon proved that the Lord not only goes with His servants, but actually goes before them. No sooner had we opened our home for meetings than a young Chinese student came along, with evidences of divine grace already at work in his heart. How did he know about us? A very intriguing story. To improve his English he had started to write to a pen-pal in Canada, who had advised him to read the English Bible with the help of a correspondence course. He had just completed his first course, and those who marked the papers told him about our meetings. He was still at high school and, once saved, began to witness to other students and bring them to the meetings and they in turn came to Christ.

Then a girl, also a high school student, started coming

as the result of a letter from a Christian relative elsewhere in Malaysia. She likewise found the Saviour and started bringing her friends to the meetings, most from heathen homes and strangers to the gospel. And so we continued: the converts brought their friends; we preached the gospel; and the Lord saved souls. We sometimes had uninvited visitors as well, the quacks of stray ducks mingling with the Chinese and English of those early meetings as two linguistic groups broke bread together.

A SEASIDE HOME FOR HIS SERVANTS

Our three children were born while we were living in Seremban—two girls and a boy. The second girl, Ruth, had a congenital heart defect, which was discovered when we arrived in Australia for our first furlough. With such poor circulation Ruth was unable to stand the cold of the approaching winter in Tasmania. So, where should we go? Like a bolt from the blue we received a letter from sunny Queensland, from a lady we had never met. She was a Mrs. Madill, and had just lost her husband, through whose ministry my old friend D. L. Craig had been led to Christ. Mr. Craig had sent her a letter of condolence explaining that Mr. Madill had a "spiritual grandson" in Australia. Hence her letter. And what did it say? Her brother had a holiday home by the seaside near Bundaberg, which he would be glad to place at our disposal.

This was our first introduction to the state of Queensland, where we now make our home.

A few years later we were back again in Bundaberg on furlough and much cast on the Lord. Ruth's health was deteriorating. Our re-entry visas, originally for one year, had been twice extended and time was running out. Were we to settle in Australia or return to Malaysia? Suddenly the Lord called Ruth to Himself, and our pathway became clear. Just at the right time we found a ship which would take us to Singapore and let us get back to Malaysia with one week to spare! It all worked out so well that we were able to rise above our sorrow and return, feeling that the Lord had called us afresh to serve Him there.

A PRIEST FINDS THE WAY

In 1969, we moved to Hong Kong, having in mind both the needs of the work there and the educational needs of our children. While settling in, we lived for a short time in a holiday home on a small island, and one afternoon the children brought along a young Italian trainee priest, a student in a nearby Roman Catholic seminary, who just seemed like ripe fruit ready to be plucked. He felt his studies were taking him further from God instead of nearer, as he had hoped. It was a sheer delight to pour into his hungering heart the great truths of Scripture, as he slipped out of the seminary and came to our home nightly during the hour allocated for watching TV. His newfound faith soon surfaced before the eyes of his superiors, and he was expelled from the seminary and sent home in disgrace. Before he left, however, we had the joy of baptizing him, afterwards linking him with some missionary friends in Italy, where he became a blessing to many. The Lord had undoubtedly led us to the right place at the right time for this unforgettable case of conversion.

THE LORD'S EVICTION NOTICE

As we continued in Hong Kong a fresh challenge presented itself in a refugee area, when the premises of the old Peace Clinic became vacant, and we began to think about moving there to start another work. Some felt it was not an ideal place to take a small family, but we kept praying, and the answer came in a most unexpected way. Our landlord gave us notice to leave the flat where we were living! He alleged he needed the flat for a relative coming from Taiwan, but we felt sure he intended to re-let the place at a much higher rent. To us, however, he was the Lord's messenger.

The premises to which we moved needed considerable renovations for the work we had in mind. Where was the money to come from? Again from an unexpected source. An aged sister in Northern Ireland had passed away and, because of some relatives who had been saved through

GUIDING, PROVIDING, ABIDING

my ministry, she had left us some money in her will. How much? Just the right amount to cover the renovations!

Thus the old clinic got a new lease of life but under a new name—On Fook Centre (*On* meaning "peace" in Chinese, and *Fook* meaning "blessing"). We turned it into a study center where high school students from the neighboring hillside shanties could come and do their homework in quietness. At the same time we gave them the gospel, and the Spirit began to work among them.

A TRUCK DRIVES HOME THE POINT

Once saved, they had no desire to hurry back to their cramped homes. So we had nightly prayer and Bible studies with them, and it was just delightful to see their progress in spiritual things. Naturally we soon had thoughts of starting a new assembly, but hesitated at first on account of another group of Christians having begun to meet in a little bungalow nearby. We therefore asked the Lord for special guidance, and it came—in singular form. A truck ran out of control on a steep hill and plowed through the bungalow, resulting in its ultimate demolition and the site becoming a garbage collection point. This left us in no doubt about what our next step should be.

As the On Fook believers continued to grow, our children were also growing, and we decided the time had come to make a home for them in Australia. Again we looked to the Lord to guide and provide, for we had put all we had into the work in Hong Kong. In which city should we settle? Where could we find a home?

Once more our heavenly Father solved the problem, and in a way which quite surprised us. While living temporarily in Brisbane, I was asked to speak at the funeral of an old sister who had always displayed a keen missionary interest. After the service, her son took me aside and enquired about our plans for the future and our need of a home. He explained that, because the city of Bundaberg was encroaching on his farm, he was going to sell some land and would soon be in a position to buy a house to put at our disposal. Here surely was a real answer to prayer, and a cause for much thanksgiving. So we settled in Bundaberg for a few years while I commuted regularly between Australia and the Far East.

AGAIN AT THE CROSSROADS

At the end of 1984, we stood at the crossroads yet again. We had always thought of returning to the mission field after our children had married and branched out in life on their own, and many possibilities were running through our minds. Malaysia? Hong Kong? Or elsewhere? There was also ample scope for an itinerant ministry throughout Australia. With such thoughts we sat

GUIDING, PROVIDING, ABIDING

down to breakfast on January 1, 1985. The phone rang—"a telegram with sad news." Bill Decker, who had built up a fruitful school work in Hong Kong, had suddenly passed away. I returned to the table in a very pensive mood because, more than once during my periodic visits to Hong Kong, Mrs. Decker had enquired about the possibility of our returning to take over the school work and allow Bill and her to retire. Things now seemed to have fallen into place, and the words of Acts 16 came forcefully to mind: *"we assuredly gathering that the Lord had called us."* With this assurance we were soon in Hong Kong again, administering the Decker Schools, and helping in other areas of work as well. Those last few years proved a real blessing to our hearts and, we believe, to others also.

We are now listed as retired missionaries, but our God has not retired, nor will He change with the passage of time. Men come and go, but He remains. Our faith takes fresh courage from His enduring faithfulness. He guides, He provides, and He abides. His mercies in the past drown out all fears about the future. *"This God is our God for ever and ever; He will be our guide even unto death"* (Ps. 48:14).

SIX

Reaping What was Sewn

In May 1952, Pearl Winterburn began the journey from her home in Ontario, Canada to a lifetime of service for the Lord in the Belgian Congo (D. R. Congo). Starting at Taraja Hospital at Nyankunde Mission Station, Pearl also labored at Lolwa, Tchabi, and several other health clinics in surrounding villages. Her story is woven with experiences of discouragement and danger—especially in a country wrought with political rebellion—as well as times of deep joy and a knowledge of His hand all along the way.

The Mouvement National Congolais party under the leadership of Patrice Lumumba became the ruling authority in the country in 1960. Lumumba, Congo's first prime minister, delivered an inflammatory message, denouncing the Belgian regime with a tirade of accusations against King Baudoiun and other government officials.

GOD IS FAITHFUL

Drunken troops roamed the streets of the capital city, Leopoldville, determined to kill the whites. Looting, raping and incredible acts of violence were the order of the day. Revenge tasted sweet to these undisciplined men.

Even in the military, discipline was non-existent. Terror reigned. No white person was safe. Whoever was not an African was a Belgian in their eyes, and their fury knew no limits.

Of course the violence and unrest soon spread from the capital city to other parts of the country. Belgians were thrown into prison or brutalized and left to die. Armed soldiers combed the streets searching for firearms and ammunition, and asking for white women. At the Lolwa mission station a missionary was accosted by a villager vowing that he would murder her and paint the fence posts with her blood. Many others had been threatened. Danger lurked everywhere.

Rebels traveling in gangs across the country would suddenly set up a road barrier and unsuspecting travelers would be violently abused.

On one occasion a breathless runner from Lolwa (75 kilometers south), brought word of a pygmy who had been gored by a buffalo. The runner pleaded with Pearl to come and help. At noon that day she left in her Peugeot station wagon, accompanied by Ernest, the school director. They found the injured man and it was obvious he needed to be taken to Nyankunde hospital. Quickly and gently they placed him in the vehicle and hurried back toward home. To their dismay, barriers had been hastily erected across the road at Komonda. Brutal hands grabbed the pygmy helper and Ernest, dragging them out of the car. Hands and sticks beat them harshly. Yelling demands for her car keys, they violently wrenched Pearl from her car. But the steering locked, preventing them from starting the car. The frustrated rebels grabbed Pearl by the hair, pushing and slapping her in their fury. It appeared they were going to drag her off somewhere! The rebels wasted no pity on the injured man in the car.

At this critical juncture a rebel superior arrived—drunk. Profanity and curses for all white people poured out of him. But suddenly he took a closer look. With a sudden change of heart he began berating the soldier who had dragged Pearl off. Thrusting his face up to Pearl he pointed at an old scar. "I remember you," Pearl said, amazed. "I stitched up that wound on your face."

In a flash he commanded, "Get in your car and go! The pygmy and your helper are beyond the next barrier. Do not stop until you see them." What an astonishing end to a terrifying encounter!

Not a soul was in sight when they arrived back at Nyankunde. Why was there no nursing staff at the surgery? She found them all earnestly praying. Word had arrived that she was being held by rebels. How they rejoiced when she entered unharmed. God had answered prayer! *"Blessed is he who has regard for the weak; the Lord delivers him in times of trouble"* (Ps. 41:1, NIV).

Alma Turnbull, *In the Heart of a Pearl There is Always Some Grit*, Markham, ON: MSC Canada, 1997, pp. 40–43.

SEVEN

When God Supplies a "Starving"

H. A. Ironside was saved in California in the late 1800's through the preaching of Donald Munro. For many years, he travelled extensively among NT assemblies throughout the United States preaching the Word. His later years were spent preaching at Moody Bible Institute in Chicago. Today, his writing continues to provide clear, biblical teaching. In this chapter, the beloved expositor tells a story on himself.

In the summer of the year 1900, my wife and I went to Bakersfield (CA) for a tent campaign...The meetings went on for two months and were blessed to the salvation of a few souls, which greatly gladdened our hearts. When the time came to take down the tent, we went over to the station to get our tickets. Just before purchasing them, a very distinct impression came to me that I should not go through to Oakland, but should stop at Fresno.

GOD IS FAITHFUL

Now I know that it is a very dangerous thing to be guided by impressions, but...the more I prayed, the less I could shake it off, so I bought a ticket for my wife to Oakland, but a ticket to Fresno for myself.

I should explain that a year before I had received a letter from a brother in the Lord from Fresno asking me, if circumstances ever permitted me to come to Fresno, to make my abode at his home...I had his address with me, and leaving my bag at the station, I went to the place indicated. What was my disappointment to learn from the neighbors that he was away for a summer vacation. I felt rebuffed and wondered whether I had not made a great mistake in following my impression.

After several days of preaching in the streets of the city, my meager funds were expended and I removed my possessions from the cheap hotel where I had been lodging. A friendly druggist allowed me to leave my suitcase in his store until I called for it.

How utterly alone I felt as I stepped out into the street! But I had a large supply of tracts so I crossed the Santa Fe tracks into what was the worst section of the city, and spent my time until two in the morning visiting the vile saloons and filthy dance halls until I had distributed about 3,000 little gospel messages. God gave the opportunity for testimony to quite a number of desperate souls.

But now the saloons were closing, my supply of tracts

WHEN GOD PROVIDES A "STARVING"

was exhausted, and I had no place to go. I tried to sleep in an empty train car, but could not get comfortable. The scripture came to me, *"My God shall supply all your need according to His riches in glory by Christ Jesus,"* and my rebellious spirit exclaimed, "Then why does He not do this?"

BENEATH THE WEEPING WILLOW

About four o'clock in the morning I decided it would be more comfortable to walk, so I headed back into town. On the grounds of the courthouse I found a large weeping willow tree, the branches of which hung very low on all sides. I crawled in under them and managed to get two hours' sleep where no one could see me.

When I awoke God was speaking to me in regard to certain things in my life concerning which I had become very careless, and I knelt beneath the tree and poured out my heart to Him. The more I confessed, the more things came to my mind which required self-judgment, until I no longer wondered why God had not undertaken for me; instead I was amazed to think how very good He had been to me in spite of my many failures...

A MESSAGE FROM HEAVEN

A little later I went to the post office to look for mail and found a letter from my step-father. As I drew the letter from the envelope, I saw a postscript staring me in the face. It read as follows: "God spoke to me through Philippians 4:19 today. He has promised to supply all our need. Some day He may see that I need a starving! If He does, He will supply that."

Oh, how real it all seemed to me then! I saw that God had been putting me through that test in order to bring me closer to Himself, and to bring me face to face with things that I had been neglecting. And so I pass this little incident on to others, hoping it may have a message for some troubled worker who may be going through a time of similar need and perplexity.

E. Schuyler English, *H. A. Ironside: Ordained of the Lord,* Grand Rapids, MI: Zondervan, 1946, pp. 97-103.

EIGHT

Two Dimes...and the Lord

Recognizing that not everyone would be able to attend a Bible School, R. E. Harlow introduced Emmaus Correspondence Courses to be used all over the globe. Today, Ed and Gertrud Harlow serve with Everyday Publications—a ministry they began more than thirty years ago to provide commentaries on the Bible in everyday English which could be easily translated or understood by people who are not native English speakers.

The bright sunshine warmed their backs as John, Ernie and Ed stood on the lawn beside the lower tennis court. Others enjoyed free time at Guelph Summer Bible School, but the trio discussed their fall program. They simply didn't have days of the week to meet all the requests for Emmaus Evening Schools.

"Fellows," Ed proposed, "we will never reach a fraction of the young people who want to study the Bible, unless we offer correspondence courses."

"What's that?" asked Ernie.

"Well," Ed explained, "you guys make up your lessons and give them to me. My wife will mimeograph them and mail them to students."

"But, how will we know if the students study them?" John asked.

"I'll make tests for each course. If we ask questions requiring answers, a student will start to think for himself."

"Sounds like a great idea," John encouraged, "I'll do mine."

"Not me," Ernie declared, "I don't want to participate. Count me out!"

Since Ernie did not agree with the other two, Ed and John proceeded alone. Ed sent notices to a number of assemblies, advertising correspondence courses.

GOD ALWAYS HAS ENOUGH

When Ed and Marg Harlow had arrived from Africa a year earlier, they bought a used Gestetner duplicator for $100. Now they needed a newer machine to prepare correspondence courses.

Ed called the Gestetner office, a British company. "Could you give me information about your new Gestetners?"

"Of course, but we have a limited supply. There are

only four left in Canada. The government has seized the remainder for the war effort. When these are gone, we can't import more until the war is over."

"What do they cost?"

"The price is $325, but you can have this machine at the demonstrator price of $300." The salesman took a deep breath and continued his sales pitch. "We will pay you full price ($100) for your trade-in. If you pay cash, you will get a 2% discount, so it will only cost you $196."

Later in the day, a delivery-man knocked at the door. "I have a machine for you. We'll pick it up in four days time unless you decide to keep it."

Like a couple of kids with a new toy, Ed and Marg typed a stencil, fastened it on the machine, inked it up and produced their first print job. The machine produced beautiful, professional looking material. But how does a missionary on a tight budget get $196 on short notice? They didn't have a tenth of that amount and as commended workers they had no guaranteed income.

The next day, the postman lifted the creaky hinge of the mail slot and deposited letters through the front door. Ed sauntered over and picked them up from the floor. A letter from The Fields office in New York caught his attention and he opened it first. Inside, he found two gifts from people he didn't know. He quickly got out a pencil, calculated the total amount and added the exchange rate. It came to $195.80. The Lord had provided. Ed threw in the two dimes to complete the $196 and, cool as a cucumber, dialed the Gestetner Company. "We'll keep the machine."

Della Letkeman, *No Time to Quit: The Biography of R. E. Harlow,* Port Colborne, ON: Everyday Publications, 2000, pp. 134–136.

NINE

God Looks After His Business

William MacDonald wrote of his friend George Campbell: *"There was something truly apostolic about his ministry. Together with his co-workers, he had seen a number of assemblies planted in Newfoundland and Labrador in the space of 30 years.....As we who knew him read the book, we will still hear his strong, earnest voice and sense afresh something of his passion for souls. But even more, we will hear a man who stood at the very gate of heaven, calling back to us to drop all the irrelevant things of life and go in for that which is eternal."*

I had been involved in the MGM* boat work for a number of years and was convinced that if one boat worked good, two would be even better. A boat came up for sale

---

* The MGM was a boat purchased from a Scottish Christian boat builder. Its original name, Margaret Grace MacKenzie, was changed to Missionary Gospel Messenger and used for many years by Herb Harris, George Campbell and others in reaching isolated coastal settlements with the gospel.

GOD IS FAITHFUL

at St. Anthony that had previously been used as a doctors' boat taking doctors and nurses to isolated villages. The boat was forty-seven feet long by thirteen feet on the beam and was a very seaworthy vessel.

Two widows, one from Vancouver and the other a friend of my family, had sent us two gifts equaling $4,500. This money came before we knew the boat was for sale. We thought it must be for a new hall in Lanse au Loup. Smaller gifts of five, ten and twenty dollars came in as well, bringing the amount to five thousand. When the boat came up for sale, we made an offer for that amount. The owners wanted more, but they accepted it. The Lord confirmed to me that we were to have the boat by giving me Psalm 89:25, *"I will set his hand also in the sea and his right hand in the rivers."*

The "Northern Light" was used extensively along the Quebec north shore and farther along the Labrador coast for nine years. Wallace Buckle was the navigator for most of those years. Men who came with us on the boat learned valuable lessons about working with other men. Things they thought they needed, like privacy and showers, they found they could do without.

We used the "Northern Light" to bring lumber and a tractor to Old Fort to use in building a hall. While we were there, we had a baptism.

One of the new believers got hit several times by people who were really upset over the baptism. Her husband, who was also baptized, put his Bible down on the ground and said, "You wouldn't dare hit my wife if I wasn't a Christian. I'd have you mopped all over the place. Just because I'm a Christian you have taken advantage of us. Let me tell you something. Before I was saved, I was a drunkard and had to be hauled in out of the snow. When I got saved, everybody was glad. Since I've been going on for God and have been baptized, we are being ridiculed. As far as I'm concerned, whether these men stay or whether these men go, I've got my Bible, I've got my Christ, and I mean to go on with the Lord, no matter what happens."

The "Northern Light" was a great asset in the work along the Quebec shore and Labrador, but I can honestly say we never got sentimental over it. That was our safeguard. If we had gotten sentimental over it, we would have had an obsolete piece of equipment on our hands when its usefulness was past. A piece of equipment is only a means to an end. It has a termination. It is not something you keep going on with. The boat provided us living accommodation when we needed it, a means of transportation from place to place and a way to carry materials we needed. It even served as a preaching platform. But methods always are changing. We don't commit ourselves to things, but to people.

GOD IS FAITHFUL

Summers on the boat were not pleasure trips. There was a lot of seasickness, dampness and personal pressures. After three or four months on a boat with a group of other men, you had nothing to hide.

Pioneer work calls for someone who will really work. Not just going out for a day or two and pitching a tent that someone else will guard, or traveling on a boat that someone else will take responsibility for—the pioneer is responsible for everything. If he makes a mistake, he is responsible for that. If he makes a hit, he is responsible for that, too. We made both. Thank God He didn't cast us off when we made mistakes. I'm thankful, too, that He gave us the grace to be humble when there was blessing following.

A man will make it or break it, depending on his vision. Often men start out and God gives them a place of blessing, and they stop there. They forget to branch out. Keep pressing on. Keep branching out. Our God is a big God and *"The Lord hath done great things for us; whereof we are glad"* (Ps. 126:3).

The same God who provided the money for the first boat provided the money for the second. He provided the crew for each of them, too. Don't box God in. Pray in faith and work with faith. Leave the results to God.

George Campbell, *Take the Challenge,* Forest Grove, OR: Good News Outreach, 1985, pp. 52-54.

TEN

We've Come to Give

R. Crawford Allison was commended from Scotland to Angola in 1935 and was later joined by his bride, Margaret. He had an excellent knowledge if Portuguese, Songo, Chokwe, Afrikaans, Shona, Chewa, Setswana and other languages and had a tremendous knowledge of African customs. Crawford and Meg served the Lord in Peso, Saurimo and in many other parts of Angola for 25 years. When they were unable to return to that country, they moved to Zimbabwe and established the first assembly in Harare in 1963. Brother Allison died in 1979.

During World War II our communications with Britain became difficult, and after the fall of Dunkirk we were completely severed so that we received no supplies and no funds. These proved to be days of real testing. Eventually we had to sell most of our clothes to obtain food for ourselves and our young child, Kenneth. Margaret was left with one dress and I had one pair of shorts and a shirt. We had come to what seemed to be the end.

Right then a letter arrived from the British Consulate in Luanda, the capital of Angola, offering to repatriate us to Scotland. We spread out the letter before the Lord and sought His guidance. In the quiet of His presence we decided to stay. We would have to decline this kind offer. God had sent us to Angola and He had not told us to leave. We would wait to see how He would provide.

AFTER THE FIRE

One of the missionaries who was retiring from the field very kindly sent overland to us a herd of milk cattle, a tremendous help in providing milk for Kenneth. God had come in to meet our need. Then came the dry season when no rain fell for several months. The entire bush country was like an oven, and the long grass became dry and dangerous. Some of the young African boys were playing in the grass near where our eight cows were foraging for feed. Without any thought of doing wrong, they set fire to the grass. Immediately, the flames roared over a vast area, trapping the cows and burning them to death.

When we came out of the house to see what had happened, we were speechless with the enormity of this loss at such a time of need. The African Christians gathered around to see what our reaction would be to this crucial loss. They stood with tears running down their cheeks, too overcome with emotion to speak. We returned to the house and fell on our knees in prayer to our sovereign Master who had sent us to this land. No words would come as we knelt on the reed mat. My Bible lay between us, and I did something I had never done before. In deep anguish of soul I opened it at random to see what would happen. Like a flash from heaven we read the words from 1 Kings 19:12, *"After the fire, a still small voice."* Yes, we were to prove that God is faithful to His servants, and was keeping account of each circumstance of our lives. We rose from our knees refreshed in our spirits and confident that we were safe in the Lord's care. Little did we know that we were also about to face another test.

MAN'S WAYS AND GOD'S

Senhor Horacio de Sa, a Portuguese trader whom I'd known well for some time, and who had come to me for dental work at various times, sent a message to the mission station for me to come down to his store to talk to him. I was ushered into a small office at the back of the store where the trader kept a large safe. He took a key and opened the safe which was literally bulging with money. He had in it thousands of pounds in Portuguese currency.

"Senhor, I know you have been cut off from your homeland these many months and nothing has been coming through to you," he said. "You have helped me in the

GOD IS FAITHFUL

past. Please take whatever you need and pay me back when you can." I was immobile, seeing so much money within my grasp yet knowing that I could take none of it. This was the severity of the test. The Scripture says, *"Owe no one anything"* (Rom. 13:8). How could I promise to pay anything back? When the trader saw my hesitancy he stooped down, filled his hands with money and tried to force me to take it. I moved away and clasped my hands behind my back. What a temptation for a Scot!

I tried as best I could to express my gratitude to my friend for his kindness. When words failed me I simply turned and headed back to the mission compound. As I climbed the hill I wondered if I had done the right thing by refusing such a kind and sincere offer. Was I being fair to my wife and child? It was a great relief to reach home and unburden my heart to Margaret and to find that she fully understood why I had responded as I did. We still had little to eat and experienced weeks of gnawing hunger. In fact the hunger pangs seemed to grow more severe after that test with the trader. Still we believed that God had promised to meet our needs and we waited for His answer. His promissory note was Psalm 91:15, *"He shall call upon Me, and I will answer him."*

One afternoon the weather was fine and we decided to take a walk down the hill from the station. Halfway down we looked up to see two visitors approaching. Margaret cried out, "Oh, my dress!" I, too, suddenly became painfully aware of my shabby attire, but there was no chance to turn back, and we went on to meet them.

As we met, the man asked, "Are you Mr. Allison?" He introduced himself, and I recognized the name of a well-known African explorer. We invited them back to our home—but with sinking hearts. How could we possibly entertain this American couple when we had not even one spoonful of tea to offer them? We sat down, and to save further embarrassment I said, "I'm sorry, folks, but we have nothing to offer you except a cup of water."

They laughed heartily. "We haven't come to take, but to give!" Then they opened their boxes and began pulling out every kind of tinned food, tinned milk and cream, and Red Rose tea bags. We had never even seen tea bags before. What a feast! This was the answer, the *"still, small voice"* for which we had been waiting. We recognized it without any doubt; our Father had spoken at last. I drank six cups of tea without stopping! The visitors had also brought clothes for Kenneth, his proper size, of course, for God makes no mistakes. We had been without quinine for many months, and here before us in a heap lay one million life-saving tablets of mepacrine, a gift from the American government. We had been going about with body temperatures of 101–$102°$ F, not ill enough to be in bed, and not fit enough to be on our feet.

GOD IS FAITHFUL

We learned that the British Consul in Luanda had told these kind folks about us, and they had made their way into the interior without delay. What touched us most was that they had enquired as to Kenneth's age and had brought him new baby clothes they paid for themselves.

The following week, on the strength of the feast, I started out on trek to visit some of the African villages. When I returned home, I spotted Margaret out on the veranda, waving excitedly to me. She pushed into my hands a cablegram that had come from New York, addressed "Allison, Angola," yet it reached us. What was this? We knew no one there. But there it was—a cablegram for the royal sum of £64. Our God had not just given us the cake, but the icing too! We never found out who sent the money, but we were convinced that it too was part of *"the still, small voice."* God had promised to meet our needs and He had done it in two ways. First, He had given us the grace to do without, then He had sent the food and the money in His own chosen time. We richly experienced the truth of Isaiah 25:9, *"Lo, this is our God; we have waited for Him, and He will save us: this is the Lord; we have waited for Him, we will be glad and rejoice in His salvation."*

R. C. Allison, *Leaves from the African Jungle,* Kilmarnock, Scotland: John Ritchie Ltd., 1999, pp. 54–57.

ELEVEN

The Burning Issue

In 1932, Ian Rathie was commended as a missionary to the Dominican Republic. After a number of years in Puerto Plata, in 1941 he and his wife, Dorothy, moved to Santo Domingo to open a new work. They started a printing press and issued Light and Life *gospel paper in the neighborhood. Then* Paths of Light, *a magazine for believers was started and later* The Dawn, *for children. These papers eventually gained circulation throughout the entire Spanish-speaking world. In Santo Domingo there was also a thriving Bible correspondence school. Many souls were saved and the assembly in Santo Domingo grew.*

I was brought up in Vancouver, Canada, in God-ordained surroundings, graduating at an early age as a school teacher. When about to apply for my first position as a teacher in the British Columbia schools, missionaries from the Dominican Republic, Mr. and Mrs. A. C. Peterkin, came to our city on furlough, making known

81

their need of a teacher for their children.

To make a long story short, I was commended by my home assembly as a teacher and helper to the missionaries, leaving home at 19 years of age.

Brother John Jenner had also been commended to the work in the Dominican Republic as a full-time worker from Victoria, BC. John and I got together to drive across the continent to New York in an old Overland touring car. The trip ended in Minneapolis, Minnesota, where I was rushed to the hospital with a ruptured appendix. In those days before antibiotics one out of ten recovered from that condition. The Lord's continued faithfulness was manifested in His healing hand so that four months later, on February 8, 1928, I landed in Santo Domingo, ostensibly to teach some missionary children for two years.

A MISSIONARY IN SPITE OF MYSELF

In my mind I had concluded that I was willing to sacrifice that space of time from my worldly ambitions and aims. I had no vision for missionary care; no audible call from on high. Yet the two years became 64 in happy, soul-satisfying proclamation of heaven's Good News to Dominican men and women, boys and girls. In great faithfulness the Lord thrust me out in spite of myself and my carnal motives, sustaining an unworthy servant for such an extended time.

THE BURNING ISSUE

At the end of this term on the field as a teacher of the missionaries' children, I made reservation on a small freighter to take me to New York. I was in Puerto Plata on the north coast, waiting to sail the following day, when I discovered that an exit permit was needed to sail, obtainable only in the capital on the south coast. Communication by telegram got the permit on a vehicle which would reach the interior city of Santiago that evening. This meant that we had to make the trip across the mountains to find the car or chauffeur. Where in that city could they be found?

After stopping for prayer outside the city, we drove down the street to see that the first car parked beside the road was the one we wanted! So a very happy passenger boarded the ship the next morning as it sailed for the United States.

Previous to this, besides teaching the missionary children, I had taken the position as English teacher for two hours a day in the local Dominican high school. However at that time the government was unable to pay teachers' salaries and was eleven months in arrears. Yet out of a blue sky, I received a check for the salary owed me. No one else in the whole country received their back pay. Now I had enough to pay my fare to Buffalo, New York, where I had arranged to meet and marry my engaged sweetheart, Dorothy Taylor.

WEDDING BELLS—AND BILLS

It was His provision at that time, and the Lord supplied every other need for that wedding in the Assembly Hall in Buffalo, from which Dorothy's mother, Nellie Atkinson, later Mrs. Cuthbert Taylor, had been commended many years previously to Angola.

Even a summer cottage in the Muskoka Lake District of northern Ontario was provided for a month long honeymoon. The "Hand that moves the universe" was clearly evident in such provisions for poor missionaries.

But if every day were cloudless, a desert would be produced. On our last Sunday evening of the honeymoon, we had gone to the dear friends' house who had loaned us the cottage. Suddenly someone appeared at the door, shouting, "The cottage is on fire!"

It was too late to save anything. All I had in my pocket was the change from a ten dollar bill resulting from a purchase that morning. Everything—many wedding presents, a good sum in cash (the result of monetary presents) went up in smoke. All Dorothy and I could whisper to each other as we watched helplessly was, *"The Lord gave, the Lord has taken away. Blessed be the name of the Lord."*

TAKEN AWAY, AND GIVEN

Job learned the great lesson: *"I know that Thou canst*

THE BURNING ISSUE

do everything." The Lord gave Job twice as much as he had before. The poor missionaries who had a fire on their honeymoon also learned it. We had arranged to sail for Santo Domingo to be there for Christmas. It seemed impossible to buy everything to replace the loss in the time available. But the money was supplied abundantly by the One who took away and then restored. Sail we did, and on time, with every loss replaced: Glory to His name!

Years later, I was invited to perform the wedding ceremony for the daughter of a son in the faith, Mariano and Pearl Gonzalez, in Chicago. After the wedding I took very ill and was rushed to the emergency ward in a nearby hospital. The diagnosis was that a heart operation was urgently needed. When told the operation would cost over $35,000, I told them I didn't have such a sum. So they moved me to the county hospital; there the operation would cost less, they said. However, after the operation was performed, and I had experienced the Lord's power to heal, I was told that the cost would be the same sum of $35,000. But in the meantime that sum had been provided by the One who fulfills His promise, *"My God shall supply all your need according to His riches in glory."*

TWELVE

Taking the Test

Born in Quebec to Scottish parents, T. D. W. Muir was born again in Hamilton, Ontario, under the preaching of John Smith and Donald Munro. He pioneered the assembly work in Detroit, Michigan.

We had a baptism at Belle Isle, an island with a commodious beach in the Detroit River. After the baptism we had to walk through long grass which on that occasion had been drenched with rain. The women folks suffered most from this for it meant that their clothing was wet. The result of such a wetting, and the long walk from the island to the street car, and the slow progress homeward, was that my wife received a severe chill which ushered in a dangerous attack of bronchitis.

For thirteen weeks she hovered between life and death, with three short intervals that made us hope for recovery, but with as many relapses, until at last a period of longer improvement ensued, and the doctor eventually said she might be allowed to get up from her sickbed.

Then came the convalescence, and, as is often the experience in such cases, she had a longing for something to tempt the jaded appetite. "If I could only have some chicken broth, I think I would enjoy it," she said. But that luxury was far from being a possibility because of my depleted purse.

THE SELL-OUT

I had a plan, however, in my mind, which I thought under the pressing circumstances offered a solution, and this I determined to resort to without telling my wife. By selling my silver watch (a gift from an uncle of mine), I hoped to manage the financial problem nicely, and this I resolved to do. But she sensed my purpose, and charged me solemnly (as I was about to leave the house) to do nothing whatever without prayer to God, and then to leave the matter with Him.

This injunction from my wife proved an effective deterrent for I realized that my purposed act would be tantamount to taking things into my own hands, and so I did not carry out my plan. But as I passed a butcher shop I saw a bargain—three pig's feet for five cents— and as the price was within my means I made what I thought was a fine purchase. Soon I had some savory soup ready for the invalid, but to my surprise, instead of being acceptable, it turned the sick patient's stomach to even think of it, and I had to eat the concoction myself to demonstrate its great palatability.

WHO FILLED THE WOODSHED?

At that time the woodshed was just as bare as our cupboard: the last block of wood was used up, and I had to scrape together the bark and splinters to feed the fire in the little stove. After I did so, I knelt down on the bare floor and told the Lord of our desperate need, and pointed out the great necessity for fuel on account of my wife's weakened condition and the danger of another relapse from being chilled. I then took the basket into the house and, as I had some business to attend to, I left this last lot of fuel in her charge to replenish the fire when necessary. I did not mention to her nor to anyone else the condition of affairs in the woodshed and went off.

On my return, she greeted me with the question, "Why didn't you tell me you had ordered a load of wood? I refused to allow the driver to deliver it because I had not heard of your doing so."

My answer was that she knew as much about it as I did, for I had certainly ordered no wood. And then I learned what had happened in my absence. The driver of a truck had come to the door to find out the location of the woodshed and to get the key to the same as he had a load of wood to deliver.

My wife told him, "There must be some mistake." But the man was not to be moved from his purpose.

"Is not this T. D. W. Muir's house?"

"Yes."

"Well, I am ordered to leave this load of wood here, and I intend to do as I was told. Show me where the woodshed is." And so he piled it in, and when I looked I saw the answer to my prayer!

TESTED AND TRIED

Soon after, a knock brought me to the front door to see a stranger, evidently a well-to-do gentleman, for from his clothes I judged him to be a man of means. In response to his enquiry I gave him my name and when he mentioned his I realized that this was a banker from upstate with whom I had had some correspondence. I welcomed him into the room and when he was seated he made enquiry about my health which I was glad to inform him was very good. Then he enquired about my wife and I told him she was fairly well now, having just recovered from a long siege of illness. While we conversed together, I saw him taking mental stock of his surroundings—the carpetless floor, the curtainless windows, and all else in keeping

TAKING THE TEST

with our early days in Detroit.

I asked him if he purposed going to the Hamilton conference, and he said, "No."

"I thought perhaps you were on your way there."

"No," he replied, and added, "There are some things in which I don't quite agree with the brethren at that conference, and that is one reason why I didn't go."

"What things, may I ask?"

"Well," he said, "Do you happen, to know Mr. B. who lives here in Detroit?"

"Yes," I answered, "And do you hold the beliefs that he holds in regard to eternal punishment?"

"Well, yes I may say I do," he replied.

"Then," said I, "I am sorry to hear it."

"Why?"

"Because such doctrines as he and you believe are totally opposed to the teaching of the Word of God."

After some further discussion, he said, "I must be going. I am glad to have seen you, and I wish you to receive this and use it in the Lord's work." As he said so he produced a roll of bills held together by a rubber band and offered it to me for my acceptance. But I withdrew my hand and said, "I cannot touch that money."

"Why not?"

"For this reason: What you have just told me severs my relationships with you. I cannot have any fellowship with one who holds the doctrine of annihilation as you do."

"But you have accepted such a gift before."

"Yes, that is true, but I did not then know that you believed these unscriptural doctrines, and so I cannot take that money."

"But," he insisted, "the money is all right, if I am not. Take it and use it."

"No," I said, "the money may be all right, but the source is not, and I cannot have anything to do with it."

"Well," said he, "if you cannot conscientiously use it for the Lord's work, nor for your own use, take it for your wife's sake, and get something for her convalescence."

"No, sir," I replied, "I cannot take your money for any purpose whatever, so long as you hold these doctrines that are opposed to the truth of God."

"All right," was his final word, "I am sorry. Goodbye." He went and that was the last I heard of him.

I closed the door and sat down, and I felt like a cad, for here was within my reach just what I required for the needs of my sick wife, and the devil said to me, "Take it, man, and use it," but the *"way of escape"* was there as well as the temptation, and the Lord gave me grace to silence the enemy. And again upon my knees I committed our cause to the God of all grace.

A SECOND CALLER

Soon there was another caller. At the side door this

TAKING THE TEST

time was a knock and when I went to answer it I found standing there a Christian woman, who had been recently saved at our gospel meetings. What do you think she brought with her? In one hand there was a pitcher filled with chicken broth, on her other arm a basket in which there was a cooked chicken, fresh vegetables, and a loaf of homemade bread. She had walked all the way from her little farm near Belle Isle bridge bearing these good things to her sister in Christ.

Again I withdrew and kneeled down to my heavenly Father who knew I had need of such things and who had so graciously turned my heartfelt prayers into heartfelt praise.

H. A. Cameron, *Reminiscences of T. D. W. Muir,* Grand Rapids, MI: Gospel Folio Press, 1939, pp. 93-97.

THIRTEEN

The Just Shall Live by Faith

Ralph J. Carter (commended from Canada in 1932) and his wife Marian (commended in 1934) were used by the Lord to establish the work in Santiago, Dominican Republic. At the beginning, stones, garbage and firecrackers were thrown at them; tracts and Bibles were burned, but the Lord's blessing on the good seed eventually came and, as of 1986 there were 17 assemblies, 20 branch works, and 52 Sunday schools in the city. Marian continued serving the Lord in Santiago after the Lord called her husband home.

Upon arrival in Santiago, I began searching for a house I could afford. I found a large, old wooden house and then waited for my furniture to arrive. As we began moving in the refrigerator it would not go through the narrow doorways of the house. First, they removed the door. It still would not fit. Next, they removed the door frame. It still would not fit. The men told me to forget it. It was impossible to move the fridge into the house.

At that moment I was thinking how much I missed my very knowledgeable and practical husband. A thought flashed into my mind. Had not the brother at the funeral reminded me of the promises to the widows. I lifted my heart to the Lord and said: "Here I am, Lord, needing Your help. I cannot believe that You have let me bring this fridge down here and not be able to use it. Please show me what to do." It came to me in a flash. Tell the men to open the refrigerator door and angle it in. It took some persuasion on my part but they finally did it. Much to their surprise, it went in perfectly well.

I NEED POWER

Because the house was rather old it was not wired for 220 volts. I called in an electrician to put in wiring for the electric stove. When he was finished he hooked up the stove. It would not work. We ended in quite an argument as he blamed my stove and I blamed his wiring. Finally, he walked off and left me with the problem. I lifted my heart to the Lord and said: "Here I am again Lord, a widow needing your help. I do not know a thing about electricity so please send someone along who does."

It was not too long before John Shannon, another missionary, knocked on my front door. I was surprised because he lived at the other end of the country and seldom came to visit me. Trying to regain my composure, I said: "The Lord surely sent you here today, John." He could sense something was wrong and asked: "What's the matter?" I explained the problem with the stove. He assured me he would check it out.

A short time later he returned. The wiring was fine and so was the stove, but the electric company had installed a meter for 110 volts rather than one for 220 volts. I had paid for the larger meter so John went to the office on my behalf. An hour later a workman arrived and changed the meter. The stove worked fine from then on. I was praising the Lord for keeping His promise to the widows.

TERMITES MOVE IN: TIME TO MOVE OUT

The house had a total of forty doors and windows which kept it well ventilated and cool. It did create, however, a bit of a problem when I had to shut them all up during heavy rains or for security purposes. The house was roomy. We had some good times during my three years there. The patio was big enough for young people's meetings, playing games or even having a picnic. The age of the house was against it, though. It was infested with termites. That made it dangerous when some of the floors started to cave in. The owner did not want to spend any money on repairs because he was hoping to tear it down and rebuild. As a result, I had to start house hunting again.

GOD IS FAITHFUL

As the Calle España Chapel was getting a bit small for us, we began thinking and praying about a building of our own. I had sold my father's house for $11,000 after he died and had dedicated the money for the building of a chapel in Santiago. While Ralph was alive we had looked at various lots but each one had difficulties. We decided it was not the right time to build. I continued to look for a lot after Ralph passed away. By the time we finally found one in 1969, the building fund had grown to $12,000.

I drew up a tentative plan for the chapel and obtained an engineer's estimate. The cost would be around $17,000. The elders wondered where we were going to get the other $5,000. The believers were not well off. They decided to write to all the assemblies in the Dominican Republic and ask them for financial help. When I heard about it, I approached the elders. I told them that my husband and I had resolved to ask no one other than the Lord for anything when we started the work in Santiago. I knew Ralph would not be pleased with what they were doing. Then I told them that I wanted to tell them a story. This is how it went:

> A pioneer preacher visited a little town called Courtenay on Vancouver Island, British Columbia, Canada. The year was 1926. He found a few Christians and gathered them together for a Bible

THE JUST SHALL LIVE BY FAITH

study. After a few months they wanted to hold regular services. They decided to build a small chapel. The preacher encouraged them. He suggested they make three specific prayer requests while the building was progressing. The first was that they would be able to open the chapel free of debt. The second, that someone working on the construction might become a Christian before the project was completed. The third request was that someone might be converted to the Lord in the first service on the opening night of the chapel.

In answer to the second prayer, a young carpenter was saved while working on the building. The answer to the first request was a little more complicated. The chapel was finished. They were cleaning it up on Saturday in preparation for the opening service on Sunday. The preacher, Mr. C. O. Bowen, informed them that there was still a $65 bill for materials that had not been paid. They all knelt on their knees in the new chapel and asked the Lord to send in that amount so that they might open debt-free. After praying together, they finished the cleaning. Everyone had left except Mr. Bowen. As he was shutting the outside gate, a lady ran up to him. Out of breath, she panted, "I have wanted to bring this to you for several days, but just could not make it. I am glad I caught you today." He thanked her and opened the envelope after she had left. Inside was $65. The Lord had answered another prayer.

The young carpenter who had been converted while working on the building played a part in the answer to the third prayer request. He had a friend of long standing that he kept inviting to the opening service of the chapel. The friend was not interested in the least. The carpenter pestered him so much that he finally said, "I'll go with you on the condition that you never ask me again." The young man replied, "All right, I'll take you on that condition to the first meeting." The friend went and that night committed his life to the Lord. The carpenter never had to invite him again, for he continued to attend all the services eagerly of his own accord.

I finished my story. I then asked the elders: "Would you like to know the name of that young man who became a Christian through his friend, the carpenter?" I paused and then I answered my own question. "His name was Ralph Carter, the man who became my husband and who started the work here in Santiago. This local church here in Santiago is really the outgrowth of those prayer meetings in Courtenay. God has not changed. He is still the same now as He was in 1926. My suggestion is that you forget all about those letters to other churches soliciting funds. Instead, we should make those same three prayer requests that those brethren in Courtenay prayed so long ago."

The elders discussed the matter and agreed to my suggestion. They probably felt that I was sticking my own neck out, because they made me the treasurer of the building fund. I took the challenge and the Lord put me to the test.

As the building progressed, we came to the end of the

$12,000. I had to go on by faith. It was a wonderful experience. Some would give me fifty cents. Others would give me a dollar or two. On Saturday I always had enough money to pay the workmen. I never had occasion to say: "Do not work any more. I cannot pay you."

The Lord definitely tried me as well. One day a bill for supplies had to be paid but there was not sufficient money in the fund. I prayed about the matter. The Lord seemed to say: "How about looking in your own purse." I quickly opened it up and, counting every last cent, I reached the amount that was due. Then I thought: "What about food for myself?" Ralph had always said to me, "Never be frightened to give to the Lord." I decided to go down and pay the bill.

GROCERIES GALORE

An hour after returning home, I heard a knock at the door. It was a lady from my English speaking Bible class. She was returning to the United States and had come to say goodbye. She chatted for a while and then said: "I have a box of groceries in the car. There is no use taking them back to the States. I brought them along thinking you could use them." I thanked her. When I opened the box later, it contained all sorts of goodies that were too expensive for me to buy. Because she was an American working for the government she had been able to buy them at their commissary.

While I was marvelling at the Lord's provision, another lady called. Several men were working in Santiago on a two-year contract. They, too, were now returning home. She left me two boxes of groceries. Others also kept coming and bringing more. In the end my kitchen was stacked with groceries and I had another seven boxes stashed in my bedroom. My needs had been met for the next three months. How good is the Lord!

EMPTY PURSE; OPENED HEAVENS

We had come to the end of the building project. I was going over the accounts. There was one unpaid bill in the amount of $50. With no money in the fund and my purse empty, I was cast on the Lord. I opened my heart and said to Him: "Lord, I have made my boast in You to these brethren. I am sure You are not going to let me down now."

A little while later a young man came to see me saying that he had not been able to give anything to the building fund because of so many other obligations. He had now fulfilled those and wanted to do his share. He passed me a check. I looked at it. The amount was $50. I went down immediately and paid the bill so that I could share with the elders the news that the building would be opened free of debt.

THE JUST SHALL LIVE BY FAITH

September 24, 1969, was the date of the opening services. It was a holiday. We had meetings throughout the day. There was a prayer meeting in the morning, Bible teaching in the afternoon and the gospel was preached at night. Two men committed their lives to the Lord in that first gospel meeting. One was the man who had painted the building. The other was an invited guest. This provided a great stimulus to the faith of all the Christians. They realized again that the Lord Jesus Christ *"...is the same yesterday, today and forever"* (Heb. 13:8).

I do hope that this experience will stimulate all those who read these lines to place their trust in God at all times and under all circumstances. I will always remember the opening of the Savica Chapel in Santiago as a day of great rejoicing.

Marian Carter, *God's Miracles to Marian: Dominican Republic 1934–1988*, Wall Township, NJ: CMML, 1995, pp. 64-70.

FOURTEEN

Escape!

Soon after Conrad and Myrtle Baehr's marriage in 1932, they began preparations to serve the Lord in China. Within a few years, the tumult of WWII and Japanese occupation of China invaded their lives. Having spent some time in Japan after the war, the hearts of Conrad and Myrtle were turned to the people of Taiwan. For the next twenty-eight years they engaged in ministry in Taiwan, pouring themselves into the Lord's work in the assembly, evangelism, literature work and producing a hymnbook.

Japan had already occupied parts of North China and was advancing up the Yangtze River valley. However, there was still some chance for travel with certain limits.

In late June the very hot season was upon us. With no fans or air conditioning at that time, those with young families needed relief. We had been asked to do the housekeeping for several such families in our summer base in Kuling. We accepted the task and left for the mountain air with supplies for the job.

Our son was just one-and-a-half years old and needed a lot of care, so we took a young farm girl, called Shih-feng, with us. She had done work for us before and was a good and faithful helper; so we were a team of four.

The Japanese were pushing upriver with gun boats. Times were desperate. Food was scarce and expensive. Toward the end of the summer the fighting near the mountains intensified, and most of our fellow workers and other summer residents hurried to get back to their work places while travel was possible. We too had plans to leave, but one day, we heard that the local Chinese officials were also leaving in fright.

HELP FOR THE HELPLESS

Conrad was worried about the many elderly and crippled missionaries and others on the mountain who could not leave. He was afraid they would be cut off without help or communication, fearing officials would cut the main telephone cable. In a moment of great concern, he ran up to the telephone office and, sure enough, there was a man with an ax, ready to cut the main cable. He quickly took charge, ordered the man to desist, and put me on the switchboard to keep the lines open among Chinese military units around the base of the mountain. He also took phones from homes (which the owners or renters

ESCAPE!

had either left to return to their bases or work, or abandoned in the crisis) to place in the homes of some of the elderly. One of these homes was Generalissimo Chiang Kai-shek's summer home!

With another missionary he made a long trip by foot to the farmlands in the valley to buy up grain and rice for those left on the mountain in case of siege. He also looked for a cow for milk supply. Walking back up the treacherous path under cover of night with many carriers behind him (plus a cow!), he suddenly heard the click of a rifle. Startled, he stopped and listened and recognized the challenge of a military guard on duty. Immediately he shined a light on his own face and answered, "I am an American—Conrad Baehr. I am bringing rice and grain for the sick and aged on the mountain" —all of this in the Chinese language, of course. The guard said, "You may pass," so Conrad and his crew returned safely with mission accomplished. Thanks to God who helped all along the perilous way and for Mr. Duff, a British missionary and merchant who handled the supply.

FINDING A WAY OUT

A young Chinese colonel eventually came to take over the protection of the area. He brought with him the heads of three Japanese officers killed in a raid and displayed them publicly near the post office. This struck fear into

GOD IS FAITHFUL

many hearts and Chinese began to leave the mountain in droves to get away, anyway they could.

We, too, decided to leave since order was somewhat restored and summer almost ended. Conrad found some lancewood poles for carrying a sedan chair. He also located carriers so that Shih-feng or I could ride and hold our son. There were six special carriers who were very anxious to be hired. They were Sinza men from the Poyang Lake region. Finding them at this time was surely of the Lord, because they had to get back to their places of work by morning. It was ideal for them and for us in every way. So we started down the steep path between the ridges.

Two walked, while two rode, praying and swaying along on any smoother bits of path covering about twenty miles that night. Sad were the sights along that trail—sights of refugees with their bundles (although some had thrown them down by the wayside) clambering down the path to get out of danger quickly. Babies were crying. Frightened small children could be seen stumbling and appeared fearful of the night with all of its eerie sounds. We recall noticing a teenager carrying his little grandmother over his shoulder while trudging on through the night. A word or two of encouragement to faith in Jesus Christ was all we could give, though we longed to talk more.

It was almost daylight when we heard the high pitched

ESCAPE!

screech of spinning wheels trying to get out of the mud. We expected to find army supply trucks bringing food products to the front lines. Conrad, alert at once, dashed off to see if he could help—no doubt hoping also to get us on one of these vehicles which might be going in our direction.

As the three of us approached the scene, there appeared to be many dead bodies lying on either side of a line of trucks. It quickly dawned on us that they were refugees, resting while the trucks maneuvered their way out of the mud, before a planned wild dash for a space on one of them. We knew there would be no room for us if or when the trucks were ready to move out. Conrad with these Sinza men ran quite a little distance to a farm house and bought five bundles of straw in order to get traction for the drive wheels. Then these men pushed the trucks out of the mud onto the roadway. Immediately the "dead folk" sprang up en masse from both sides and piled into the trucks.

What a crowd! We watched in dismay—and yet not hopelessly, for we were constantly looking to the Lord to make a way for us. Gunfire echoed in the distance and some plane activity had begun overhead. The driver of the first vehicle came over and said to Conrad, "You folks get into the cab with me." God's marvelous provision before our eyes! Quickly we squeezed in—Shih-feng was literally thrown on top of the load in the back of the open truck. She must have wiggled down with her little feet trying to find something firm. When we looked back, there she was, smiling, although pressed on every side by bodies.

We lumbered off ever so thankful. Once along the roadside, however, we all had to jump out and run for cover into the fields, because enemy planes were following, hovering over us. The driver was afraid we would be their next target, since we were out in the open. After a while we all climbed into the truck again. The driver intended to leave us at the train station, but having heard that it had been bombed the day before, we begged him to take us further along to his next stop. How relieved we were to hear him say, "I'll take you beyond—a safe distance."

Prayer and praise occupied us as we went along. Conrad was "talking the gospel" to the driver. Then someone died in the back en route, so his body had to be ejected. Normally this would be a terrible act for Chinese, but no one argued with the driver. At every stop, we checked on Shih-feng and, bless her heart, there she was still smiling.

At a hut for dressing the wounds of soldiers in battle, the driver stopped and told us all to get off. We four took refuge from the sun in the hut. Our baby Kingsley was really suffering with the heat, a rash, and perspiration.

Shih-feng said, "Let me take him to that house over there by the stream. I'll wash him and get him into the shade." We said, "Yes, but hurry back in case another truck comes by and maybe we can ride further on."

STRAFED BUT SAFE

They were not gone long when planes roared overhead. The soldiers cautiously peeked out, then turned to yell ecstatically, "Chinese planes!" The wounded men all around us with bandages very evident then hurried outside to wave wildly. They saw the Chinese insignia under the wings! Suddenly, the planes banked around, and they saw on top of each wing the red ball of Japan! Everyone yelled, "Hide! Quick!"

Worried and excited in the extreme, we looked for Shih-feng and our baby. Yes, there she was, running with him under some trees. We yelled and motioned for her to hurry, needlessly, of course. The Lord answered our prayers, and soon they were by our side. The soldiers around us warned that the planes were returning and yelled again for all to hide. Connie took Kingsley and covered him with his own body, drawing a big tray of rice bowls over the top of them both. I was frozen to the spot. Strafing from the low-flying planes began to focus on our hut. One or two of the soldiers were killed. The refugees rushed outside to scatter. My ear began stinging severely.

We guessed a piece of shrapnel had come almost too close!

During a lull, Shih-feng and I ran out back, headed for some low-hanging bushes along what appeared to be a stream.

All four of us found ourselves together under branches on a mud bank. We softly sang about the True Refuge once we got settled and quiet. Did I say "quiet?" With the noise, the tension, and the wild clamor all around, Kingsley was crying so loudly it seemed that even the fliers would hear him. We prayed, earnestly asking our Lord's help. He did not delay!

Suddenly, out of the slimy mud, tiny green frogs began jumping around. Kingsley's attention was riveted on them. His crying stopped and there we were, down in the mud, singing lines from "Jesus, Lover of My Soul,"

> *Other refuge have I none,*
> *Hangs my helpless soul on Thee...*

After an hour or so, the planes left that area, and we found a truck to continue our journey another forty miles beyond.

OUR DECISION: GOD'S PROVISION

We had been away from our homeland over five years and felt that we could take a furlough at this time. Myrtle

ESCAPE!

assured me that she had combed Shanghai's travel agencies to register us for passage to the United States, but to no avail. The word on the street was, "White Russians and others are leaving for America in great numbers." There was nothing available.

Several days later, Myrtle went out with Kingsley for a walk. Unexpectedly, she met a missionary friend, Ruth, from another mission group. Each was very surprised to meet the other. Ruth asked, "Are you leaving like everyone else?"

Myrtle's response was a dull, "No, we can't find a ship to take us." Ruth's face lit up as she responded, I have a booking for two to leave the day after tomorrow, but I can't go now. My fellow worker is quite ill and I can't leave her. Can you leave right away?"

You can imagine the reply! We had no money to pay for the tickets, but that did not seem to bother Ruth. We arranged to send her the amount immediately upon our arrival in New Jersey.

Our glorious Lord never fails to keep His promises.

That very night, a girl came looking for Myrtle and bringing a letter. It had been delivered to her parents' home several days before, but they had been delayed in getting it to us. In it was a check from our home assembly at Grove Street Chapel for enough to cover passage for two to the United States! We were so enraptured by

His provision that we could hardly sleep. Seeing His hand all along the way, we were reassured that our unplanned furlough was in line with His will.

Conrad and Myrtle Baehr, *Campaigning for Christ,* self-published, 1998, pp. 59–64; 71–72.

FIFTEEN

Our Daily Bread

Christopher Willis, with his wife and three little children, went to China in 1921. They lived and labored first in the South and later in the central part of China, but the greater part of the time he was in charge of the the Christian Book Room of Shanghai. During World War II, they were held captive in a Japanese concentration camp.

We had not been in concentration camp many days before it was apparent that in all this great company of Britishers, there was scarcely a trace of any recognition or acknowledgment of God. The vast majority appeared to have little or no care for their Maker. Amongst those who took upon themselves the Name of Christ, there was a great dividing line, separating a little remnant who believed implicitly in the Word of God, from the large majority who seemed more occupied with what they did not believe than anything else.

Included in that little remnant, who were drawn so closely together, were Mr. and Mrs. P., and their daughter C., about fourteen, but even at that age taller than either of her parents. Mr. P. was an old friend, whom we had known and loved for many years. Then there was Mrs. S., a stranger to us, but not a stranger for long. She was older than the rest of us, and was on her way home to be retired, when she was caught by the war; and how thankful many were that God had so ordered her pathway! She and her husband had done noble pioneer work in North China. He had died many years before from a heart attack, after baptizing a number of new converts. He had suffered much for Christ's sake, so breaking down his health; and Mrs. S. herself knew what it meant to be beaten for His Name. There were few to whom we were all so greatly drawn as to this dear saint, and one of the joys and compensations for those years in camp was to learn to know her.

There were others whom I would gladly name, but from the beginning the few mentioned met each Saturday evening in our room, and there we poured out our hearts together, telling our Lord of the things about us that grieved us so very much.

GOD SUPPLIES OUR NEEDS

In the old days, before the war, one of our interests in the Book Room was to make illuminated Scripture texts.

OUR DAILY BREAD

This part of our business had grown to such an extent that our artist was kept busy all the time. When Japan attacked the British and Americans, and we had to let our men go, the artist went to his home in Kashing, a hundred miles or so from Shanghai. We still had a few orders for texts come through, and the work of preparing them fell to me.

We had about half a roll of drawing paper on hand, but one day on my way home from work, it seemed as though a voice said: "Go and buy drawing paper." I was not disobedient to the call, and immediately went to the supply shop where I always dealt. I purchased two rolls, twenty yards each, for a little less than $80.00. Not many weeks later the same shop was asking $600 a roll. I also was compelled to buy more paints, which rather vexed me, as money was generally short. We only used British-made paints, as they stood the sun better than those made in China. The only British paints available were in large tubes, and cost a lot of money. As these tubes were so hard to sell, the shop kindly gave them to me at a very low figure. A few weeks later they were almost priceless. I bought several slabs of an excellent quality Chinese ink, specially wrapped, and printed "For Export." But as there was no export then, these were also being sold at a very low price. I bought a supply of the best Chinese brushes I could get, and so was ready to do the odd text in place of our artist. I did not know that all this was God's provi-

GOD IS FAITHFUL

sion for life in camp. But all these things I brought with me, except one roll of paper which I left with a Chinese friend, and had forwarded a year or so later to the camp.

A SILENT WITNESS

As we grieved and prayed over the conditions of the camp, the thought came to me that a text might speak, even though there was no opportunity for our lips to speak for Christ in public; and with an utter lack of privacy anywhere, it was hard to carry on a serious conversation even with an individual. The dining room seemed the best place for such a text to be displayed. There was a large Gothic window in the end of the room, high up off the floor. Just below this window, facing the whole room, seemed the ideal place to put it. I well knew the storm it would raise, and for that reason we made it a special matter of prayer that just the right words might be given us. The text selected read:

> Our Father
> Which art in heaven
> Hallowed be Thy Name
>
> Give us this day our daily bread

The text was, as I recall, almost five feet long and not quite three feet high. It was done in blue, crimson and gold with the letters shaded with brown. The letters were Old English and the capitals Gothic. The only place to work was on my bed, but I had an old drawing board and that was a great help.

We knew that it was useless to ask permission from the Camp Committee to put up such a text. They would never have granted it. So night by night as the work on the text progressed, done in secret as far as possible, the little company of believers met for prayer that the Lord would undertake and over-rule so that the text might go up in the place selected, and that none might be able to move it. How God abundantly answered those prayers, in a way more than we could ask or think, the rest of the story will tell.

It took a little over three weeks to finish the text. I was anxious that it should first appear on a Sunday morning. By Saturday evening, at supper time, there was only two or three hours' work left: so, as our chairman, Mr. Grant, was eating his supper, I asked him what time he got up in the morning. I think he thought me very impertinent, but graciously replied that he was up every morning by six; so I asked him if he could meet me in the dining room the next day a few minutes after six. He agreed, and I hastened back to try and have my text ready in time. The little company gathered as usual to specially commend it to the Lord's own care as it started out on what we knew

GOD IS FAITHFUL

would be a stormy course. Just as I put the last strokes to the text, suddenly I spilled two great smears of black ink right across one end, on top of quite a few of the letters. It was just roll-call time, and then all lights were out.

I was almost in despair, but knew that my drawing paper was extremely good, and would stand a lot of rubbing. We lit a candle, and for an hour or more worked at it until the damage was repaired, and the mess could not be detected. We occasionally tried to light a candle for some special need at night after that, but always the guards shouted at us, and aimed their searchlights into our room. Indeed, one night they came up with their heavy boots and their guns, and I don't know what they would have done to us, only they missed the room, and went to our neighbor's door. They kept their door locked, and were so sound asleep that the guards gave it up as a bad job. There was of course no light then to be seen anywhere. But on the night we had to fix the text, we had no trouble at all, nor indeed did we know we were not supposed to have a light if we needed it.

The next morning about half-past five, I was down in the dining room and got the text well pinned up with thumb tacks. Mr. Grant came in shortly afterwards, and I watched to see what the verdict would be. I knew he was a fair and honorable man and I knew I would get a much more sympathetic hearing from him than from the Camp

Council. He did not speak for a few minutes, looking with care at it. At last I asked: "May it stay?"

VARIED REACTIONS

He waited again, and then replied: "Why not? Yes, it may stay. It is reverent, and it is well done. It may stay."

I decided to strike while the iron was hot, and asked: "May I do one for the other end of the room as well?"

"Yes," he replied, "do one for there also. And come into the office where you will have room and a table to work on, and do it there." I could only bow in thanksgiving, as Mr. Grant returned to his room.

My duties were cutting the bread for breakfast, which often meant a start at five-thirty; and then pouring water and tea for breakfast. The new text was just over our heads. It was intensely interesting to hear the comments as we poured. "What's this?" "Who's done this?" "Take it down!" "Oh, it's only up because today's Sunday, it'll be down tomorrow; don't bother with it." "Who put that up without permission?" "We'll soon see about that." And very occasionally a remark of appreciation by someone who loved or honored the Word of God.

One person said, "You can't have a text like that up in this camp; there's too much swearing." It is true the foul language was terrible, but I could only remark that I could not see that this was a sound reason for taking down the text. If it was true that the text and the swearing did not go together, why not give up the swearing?

I had asked Mr. Grant not to mention who had done it, and for several days it remained a secret. As anticipated, it caused a great commotion. The Camp Committee discussed it, and disapproved of it, because of the offense it would give to the Catholics and the Jews. The Catholics replied, by their leader coming to me. He said: "There's just one thing wrong with that text."

"What is that?" I asked.

"It needs a frame. If you'll find the wood, I'm a carpenter and will make the frame, and then they'll all know it's not the Catholics who object to the text." The only wood available was a slice off the frame of my bed, but it was very hard wood, and polished quite nicely.

The Jews sent over a little committee of three with their prayer book, to show that every word in the text is in their prayer book, and to say that they liked the text and hoped it might stay. So the "reasons" of the Council faded out.

Again the question came up in the committee, and very strong words against it were uttered, trying to force it to be taken down. Mr. Grant was about to try and defend it, when a business lady on the Council took the floor. I was not present, but was told that by the time she had finished telling the opposers what she thought of them, there was not one who dared to say another word. And once again we bowed in thanksgiving. But a text for the other end of the room was prohibited.

NO TEXT, NO BREAD

It might have been several months after this, and everybody had grown used to the text, when it was decided to have a play. This was held in the dining room, with the tables from the bakery (good heavy ones) arranged as a stage, just under the text. Somehow they felt this did not fit in very well with the play, so they took it down and stuck it in a corner of the room. Next morning the room was cleared up, the tables taken back to the bakery, but the text was left in the corner of the room.

When I came to cut the morning bread that day, the sad reply was: "No bread ration today; the bakery's failed us." (I think the flour had failed). The bread was very truly our staff of life, and with nothing as a substitute, we were hungry indeed. Many a night even before that I had awakened with hunger, and was unable to get to sleep for hours: but now it was worse. Everybody felt it, and the next day was the same.

When the third day came and still no bread, the murmurings broke out, and all over the camp one might hear: "It's because of that text. They've taken down the text, 'Give us this day our daily bread,' and since then we haven't had any bread." Another was heard to say, "That text is our mascot. We must get it up again."

The feeling in camp was running so high, and we were all so hungry, that finally the very ones who took down the text, were compelled to put it back again.

WILL THEY EVER LEARN?

Several months went by, and once more the camp held a play. The arrangement was as before, but this time heavy curtains were draped in front of the text, and on the curtains was pinned a very well drawn picture of a pair of balances, and a sword, representing "justice." The day following everything was cleared up except the curtains, with the picture of the balances and the sword still pinned to them, so that the text did not appear.

Again, there was no bread. I think this time the yeast failed to come, but when we came for our usual ration, we were met with the sad news: "No bread today."

During the course of that day, as we were compelled to be occupied with the balances and sword, my wife remarked that the picture presented a remarkably good opportunity that we ought not to let pass—so the next morning when we came down for breakfast rations (but without any bread), there appeared above the balances and sword the lines:

OUR DAILY BREAD
TEKEL
"Thou art weighed in the balances, and art found wanting"
Daniel 5:27

I saw Mr. Grant chuckle as he went up to get his breakfast, and he whispered to me as he passed: "I see you are an opportunist."

I replied, "You understand it?"

"O yes, I understand it perfectly," he replied. But as you can guess, most of the camp was not as well pleased as Mr. Grant. The whole camp was angry that once more they were without bread, and the demand came on every side, "Take down the curtain!" Once again the enemies of the Truth were compelled to surrender, and the curtains came down, leaving the old text with full possession, and the bread came to us once more.

THREE STRIKES

Some months later, for a third time, the text was again taken down, and this time thrown behind the piano. Again, the same day, the bread failed; and finally a gentleman in camp, who had been manager of a large brewery, came to me with the suggestion: "That text should be nailed up, so they cannot take it down."

I replied: "I know you are very handy with tools, suppose you nail it up?"

GOD IS FAITHFUL

"Gladly," he replied; and with great long nails the text was finally nailed up so that nobody again ventured to touch it, and it was still there until camp was broken up, ever uttering its silent prayer:

"GIVE US THIS DAY OUR DAILY BREAD"

And the bread never failed again.

G. Christopher Willis, *I Was Among the Captives: Life in a Japanese Concentration Camp,* Singapore: Christian Book Room, n.d., pp. 84-89.

SIXTEEN

Step by Step

Charles Stanley (1821-1890), of Rotherham, England, was left an orphan at the age of four. Converted when fourteen, that year he preached his first message. At age twenty-three, with meager capital, he began his own hardware business in Sheffield. As a salesman, he crisscrossed England, at the same time doing "the work of an evangelist." Forty years later, he said, "Seldom in those days did the Lord open my lips without some soul being converted. Not that this appeared at the time, but I have met them everywhere, ten, twenty, or thirty years after."

The city of York had been on my mind for some months, and I had often looked to the Lord in prayer about it. I was returning home one day from Scarborough, and had about three hours to wait at York. As I walked over the bridge, I lifted up my heart in prayer and asked the Lord if it were His will that I should preach the Word there, to give me a congregation that day. While I was in prayer, I met a great crowd turning down by the castle. The Lord said, "Follow this crowd." I found there was going to be a funeral of some Roman Catholic dignitary. We walked on until we came to a large shed. The rain fell at this moment, and the people rushed in and filled the shed.

I felt it was the Lord's will I should stand in front of the shed. I took out my Bible and read the words, *"Blessed are the dead which die in the Lord."* A very large company gathered in front. Some hundreds heard the Word with marked attention. The Roman Catholics seemed to think I was one of themselves, and, crossing themselves, came very close. I was led to dwell first on the blessedness of those who now fall asleep in Christ. I did not refer to the special time to which this text applies, but, as a general fact, how blessed is the soul that departs from this scene to be with the Lord. I then showed that the Word did not say, "Blessed are they that die in the Roman Catholic church, or in the Protestant churches, but IN THE LORD. This caused rather a flutter, and then even greater attention, while I endeavored to show from Scripture, what it was to be *"in the Lord."*

As I closed, a man asked me in a distinct, clear voice that was heard by all, "Do I understand you to say that a man may know in this world that he is saved, and that he has eternal life?"

This question, and the answer, appeared to have great effect on many as I showed from Scripture that it was the privilege of all believers to know that they were *"justified from all things,"* and had peace with God. For the Word says, *"Be it known unto you, therefore, men and brethren, that through this Man is preached unto you the forgiveness of sins; and by Him, all that believe are justified from all things."* If we believe God, how can we doubt it when He says *"Be it known unto you"*? Other scriptures were quoted, and just as I finished my answer, the head of the funeral approached us, being about two hours behind time. Let us not say this was strange; it would not be so at all if we walked more in faith.

THE ONLY TRUE DOCTRINE

I was walking with a friend one Lord's Day morning at Newcastle, in the Potteries. My friend said, "The man we are meeting is a very earnest, devoted Roman Catholic."

I turned aside to him, and said, "Here, I want you for a particular matter this afternoon. I want you to make known to the Roman Catholics that I hope to preach in the market at three o'clock today, and mind you let them know that I am about to prove that the doctrine of the Church of Rome in the year 60 is the only true doctrine."

"I quite understand," said he.

"And," I continued, "see that they all stand as near me

GOD IS FAITHFUL

as they can get, and that they don't let anyone disturb or hinder me from going through the discourse."

It was astonishing what a number of them were there by three o'clock; and they stood packed all round, so that no one could get at me. I then commenced, and showed that we were not left in any uncertainty as to which was the true church at Rome in the year 60. It was composed of all the believers in Rome—the one church, the only true one church at Rome. Neither were we left in any uncertainty as to what were the true doctrines of the church at Rome in the year 60. We have an inspired account of those doctrines, and to that document we turned our attention.

From chapters 1 to 3 we found the statement as to the total ruin of man through sin. Whether Jews or Gentiles, all were sinners, all guilty, all utterly unable to acquire righteousness by works of law. Every man found it so, also, by his own experience. It must be so, for this was the true doctrine on the subject of the church at Rome in the year 60; and it was the only true church in the year 60 at Rome. There was no other.

I then went on to show God's righteousness revealed in the glorious plan of redemption. How He is righteous through the atoning death of Jesus, in justifying all that believe Him. *"Their faith is reckoned for righteousness"* (ch. 4). Believing God, *"who raised up Jesus our Lord from the dead, who was delivered for our iniquities, and was raised again for our justification."* They are thus accounted righteous, justified. I gave illustrations of these, to show that the mighty debt of our sins had been paid; and the everlasting proof was Jesus risen from the dead. He is our everlasting righteousness.

This being the case, there was one striking peculiarity of the church at Rome, or the believers at Rome. A mark of the true doctrine was this, that they did not hope to be saved. They did not hope to make their peace with God. They HAD peace with God. *"Therefore being justified by faith, we have peace with God, through our Lord Jesus Christ."* Here is the true doctrine of the church at Rome in the year 60. All doctrine contrary to this is heresy and falsehood. The utter corruption of human nature; all guilty. Redemption through the blood of Christ, not human works, is the remedy. All that believe God are justified, and have peace with Him—are not hoping to make their peace with God. Jesus has finished the work on the cross. They believe it, and have peace with God through Jesus Christ.

Well, the application began to be too pointed for my friends. They looked at each other, as I asked if this was the doctrine of those around me. Had they found that they were utterly lost sinners, and that, try as they might, they could not acquire righteousness or peace by works of law? Had they accepted this full salvation through Jesus Christ? Did they really believe God? Were they hoping to get peace, or could they say with the Roman believers in the year 60, *"We have peace with God"*? I assured them there was no salvation apart from the doctrine of the church of Rome, as revealed in this epistle in the year 60.

By this time some of my inside friends had become outsiders, and some had disappeared, but many listened to the end; and I had not an insulting word. Oh, may the day declare that souls were that day brought to rest in Christ, and believed the Word of God.

Charles Stanley, *Incidents of Gospel Work or The Way the Lord Hath Led Me,* Hong Kong: Christian Book Room, n.d., pp. 31-33, 77-80.

SEVENTEEN

Provider and Protector

Abigail Townsend Luffe was raised in England and as a young girl was impacted by the faith of her father's friend, George Müller. His lessons of the prayer-hearing, prayer-answering God followed her to Buffalo, New York, where her own life proved the Lord's faithfulness. She trusted Him to provide a home for elderly saints.

In the summer of 1921, very early one morning while in prayer, the need of more room was forced upon me by the Holy Spirit, in the following words, *"Enlarge the place of thy tent and let them stretch forth the curtains of thine habitation: spare not, lengthen thy cords, and strengthen thy stakes"* (Isa. 54:2). I cried out, "O, Lord! What can I do?"

Quickly the answer came, *"Fear not, for thou shalt not be put to shame, neither be thou confounded...in righteousness shalt thou be established"* (Isa. 54:4, 14). I then knew the Lord meant me to trust Him for a new home. I asked Him to impress upon my mind how much I should pay, either for a house or to build, for, as yet, I did not know which He would lead me to do. The sum of $30,000 was impressed upon my mind. Then I asked the Lord if I were to buy a house, would He show me the house by having one brought to my notice, which would be thoroughly renovated.

HEAVEN'S ANSWER IN THE MAIL

The morning mail brought me nine letters, four of which contained money.

The first one I opened was from a little girl who was dying. The letter contained a $10.00 bill. Her letter said the doctor told her she could not live many days and she had hoped to make the gift much larger, but that was the most she could give. She hoped that it would be put in the foundation stone of a new home. She had heard from the area ministers how badly I needed a new home.

Another letter contained a check for $25.00 from a person who had never contributed to my work before nor who has ever contributed a cent since. The writer said he wished it might be used in the purchase of a new home for my work.

Another letter contained a check for $50.00 and the sender wrote: "How I wished you were buying a new home and this money could be used for the fund."

A fourth letter contained a check for $15.00. The sum total of the money received in that mail was $100.00.

This convinced me that I was to go out and buy a home.

My co-workers said, "If you are going to buy a home at once, we will do the work."

I started out at once to find a reliable agent. I called on Mr. —, a well-known businessman of Buffalo, for advice as to whom I might go. I went to the agent recommended by him, saying that I wished to buy a suitable house for invalids.

He asked, "How much money have you?"

I replied "$100.00."

He looked at me in astonishment. "What locality?"

"The North Circle." He was still more astonished, as this was one of the most aristocratic sections of Buffalo, having two multi-millionaires living on adjacent corners.

Striking his knee with his fist, he said, "A good many people would like to buy a house in that location with only $100.00," and further remarked, "That's strange, I received a message telling me that there is a house on the North Circle for sale. It is the first time that I have ever had a house for sale on the North Circle and I am not sure of it yet, as it was only a message over the phone."

I asked him for the number of this house on the Circle

and he replied that it was 26 Richmond Avenue. I was rather startled, and told him so, for it was the house that I had often called *my* house. The much handsomer houses and the prettier houses never attracted me like that large one on that corner, and in my heart I said, "After all, can it be that my poor suffering saints are to have this house for a home?"

The agent said that he would come on Monday and report all conditions to me about this matter.

I said, "No, no, this matter must be settled today." He demurred about it, but I said, "If you cannot go, I will go myself and find out what I want to know."

Fearing to lose his commission if I did this, he said he would go, but I could see it was very reluctantly. He said it would place him in a very awkward position as he did not even know the name of the owner.

I said, "I will save you any embarrassment if you will allow me to be the first speaker."

In answer to the ring, a lady opened the door. I said, "Are you the lady who wished to sell this house?"

She answered, "Yes."

I said, "I have not the pleasure of knowing your name. I am Mrs. Luffe and yours?"

"Mrs. Eugene Howard."

"Making this call without an appointment, I have made it most embarrassing to the agent, as he was not acquainted with your name, but my reason for coming is that I expect to leave Buffalo for a six weeks' trip Monday morning. May I tell you a little story about why I want this house?" She quite graciously assented. I told her of the work of faith that God had used me for during the last twenty years in Buffalo. I told her that I had been brought up and trained in the work of faith by my parents, and I was sure God had called me out to do a larger work, recounting to her the morning's occurrences.

She asked me if I had any idea what the house would cost.

I said, "No."

"How much money can you put down?" she asked.

"At present only $100.00, to secure an option of the house."

"Have you any idea of the value of this home?"

"Will you tell me how much you can give for it?"

"I prefer for you to state your price." I replied, "One condition that I have in mind is, that the house I purchase must be in full repair."

She replied that this house had been recently renovated from the outside of the roof to the inside of the furnace. Mrs. Howard was very thoughtful for a few moments in which neither of us spoke a word. She then said, "I would very much like this house to be used for just such a work, but I could not possibly let it go for less than $26,000.00. Are you, afraid of this?"

"No, not in the least," I answered.

"I would have to have $1,000.00 on the first of September to bind the contract, $6,000.00 on the first of October, when the deed would be passed. There is a mortgage of $6,000.00, which you would have to pay, and a second mortgage for $19,000 to be paid in semi-annual installments of $750.00."

I urged her to allow me to pay $2,000.00 a year, but she feared it would be too much, as I would have to pay interest on both mortgages.

She said, "I will give you the option on this house until you return, but will not take your $100.00."

On the following Monday morning, while waiting for a car to take me to the railroad station for my six weeks' trip, I was met by the postman, who handed me a special registered letter. Upon opening this letter on the train, I found $1,000.00 in War Savings Stamps, just the money needed for the first payment. This was to be put away until I was ready to use it for the home. What a wonderful God we have, who considers all details in the lives of His children.

THE RIVER FLOWS ON

At the conference to which I went, I told them about the house the Lord had given me for the blind and lame and aged. *"Out of the abundance of the heart the mouth speaketh."* You know, I had to speak, for my heart was brimming over.

A lady whom I had never seen nor heard about, said to me, "How much coal do you expect to burn? I should like to pay for this year's coal."

Thanking her, I said, "The coal is already in the cellar of the new house."

I had already ordered my coal to be put in my home at 257 Plymouth Avenue, but I asked the owner of this house to put the coal at 26 Richmond Avenue. To this she assented.

"Have you received the bill?"

"Yes, it came this morning." She thereupon wrote me a check for the amount.

A few days after, a farmer came to me and asked me, "Will you not need a telephone? How much is it in Buffalo?" Telling him the amount, he paid me one year's telephone bill.

A dear little boy gave me two cents out of five he had for candy. Another boy gave me twenty-five cents from his holiday money, also, one dollar which he earned by selling bread. Never once did I mention the need of money, but the Lord knew, and *"He sat over against the treasury."*

On the first of September, according to agreement, I

GOD IS FAITHFUL

met the lady, paid the $1,000.00 and the contract was signed.

A short time before October 1, word came from the owner asking how well I was prepared to meet this payment of $6,000.00 on that date, saying that if it would be a help to me and be convenient for me to pay it, $5,000.00 would be accepted and the deed would be passed as she had a good opportunity for investing the money.

The day arrived for the payment of the $5,000.00. At nine o'clock in the morning I was $1,500.00 short, as men say. One can imagine my tenseness and the test of faith, more especially fearing that I was running before the Lord in accepting the alteration in the payment day.

Twenty minutes past nine came, when a special delivery was received with a check for $1,000.00, the donor of this check being under the impression that this was the day first agreed upon when the deed was to be passed. How wonderful is God to know that the date was changed, and to lead this person to send this check just in time. He is able to do these things for those who trust him. Half past nine came, with $500.00 still lacking.

At twenty minutes to ten, I started out for the lawyer's office, Sister Iona accompanying me. Halfway down the steps the postman came round the corner and handed me a letter, saying, "That is a poor skinny letter and only one today." I said, "Wait and see; I am praying for $500. We will see if it is in here." Opening the letter, there it was.

So foolish was I that it never occurred to me to put the money in the bank and draw a check, but just as the money had been given to me, from the two cents given by the little boy at the conference, the first money received after the War Savings Stamps—to the last check of $500.00, I carried the money to the lawyer's office in a bag and poured the five thousand dollars into Mrs. Howard's lap. I never saw such an amazed group of people as the little packets and envelopes were opened, each containing someone's gift. Many of my friends thought that a few rich people would come forward and pay for the home outright, but that would not have been such a testimony to God's way of doing things as this remarkable occurrence. I really believe they thought I was crazy, but it was God's way, for He led me to tell just how the money came.

THE PICKPOCKETS

Just to let thy Father do
What He will;
Just to know that He is true
And be still;
Just to follow, hour by hour,
As He leadeth;
Just to draw the moment's power

GOD IS FAITHFUL

As it needeth;
Just to trust Him, this is all!
Then the day will surely be
Peaceful, whatso'er befall,
Bright and blessed, calm and free.

Thus mused Sister Abigail as she started home from a visit to her sister. She had planned to go home much earlier, but found so many little things she could do for her comfort that she was hindered and now darkness had fallen. But Sister Abigail had long ago learned that often the hindering things brought the greatest measure of blessing. So as she hurried homeward through the darkness she rested in faith that the delay was part of God's plan for the day, for had she not committed the day to Him?

When she reached the corner of a certain street she quickened her steps, remembering the street was poorly lighted and that she must pass two vacant lots. Just as she reached this dark place, suddenly her hands were pinned behind her, and a husky voice said, "What do you have in your bag, lady?"

With a cry of prayer to God for help, Sister Abigail said, holding up her Bible, as her hand was free, "I will give you this; it is the most valuable thing I possess, for it says, *"For God so loved the world, that He gave His only begotten Son, that whosoever…whosoever…whoso-*

ever..." Being paralyzed with fright, she lost the power of speech, but again endeavored to say, *"Whosoever believeth..."* The third time she attempted to finish *"whosoever,"* the thief was so angered that he grasped her by the neck of her coat, and shook her as a cat would a rat, pushed her off the sidewalk toward a snowbank, and sped off through the darkness.

Sister Abigail tremblingly hurried home, and special prayer was asked for the unknown pickpocket.

But does it pay to pray?

WHOSOEVER

Four years passed. Sister Abigail still kept the pickpocket on her prayer list and continued to ask that the Word sown would bear fruit.

A few days before Easter she went with one of her helpers to do some shopping. She hoped before returning home to call on a young girl whom she had often invited to come to her house. The girl had always made the excuse for not coming that she did not know how to get there. So Sister Abigail took a small card on which was printed two texts of scripture, and wrote around the edge her name, address, what trolley car to take and where to alight, to reach her home. Folding this up, she tucked it into her change purse.

But surely God directed her hand as she selected the

card. "By myriad paths He leads His children home," and He knew, if Sister Abigail did not, who would read that little card.

When the shopping was completed, she found it was too late to make the call, so they boarded a trolley car for home. This incident occurred when the cars were in use where the passengers placed the right fare in a box at the front of the car. As Sister Abigail reached up to drop her fare into the box, two men pushed roughly against her, but she gave no special thought to them.

On reaching home, she found some additional purchases needed, so opening her bag to get her purse, she found it empty. The purse was gone.

There was no fret, no worry over the loss, as our sister truly believed that *"All things work together for good to them that love God."*

The next morning while the family were at prayers, a ring at the door was heard. Being answered by one of the helpers, she returned stating that a man wished to see Sister Abigail.

Thinking that he might be a book agent, and being very busy at that hour in the morning, she sent word to that effect, and requested that he make his errand known to the helper. He replied that he must see Mrs. Luffe and see her alone. He was then admitted to the little sitting room, the others being asked to retire.

As he entered the room, he asked, "Did you lose your purse yesterday?"

"Yes," she replied, "but what do you know about that?" She arose to cross the room as she put this question, and the man gave a sharp, sudden look at her.

He again asked, "Were you held up on Tracy Street one night about four years ago?"

Sister Abigail, greatly astonished, answered, "Yes, but what do you know about that?"

"Well, lady," he replied, "I am the man that stole your purse and I am the man that held you up. I took your purse when you reached up to put your fare in the box. I have come to give myself up, and want you to call the police. I am through with this life." One can scarcely imagine the surprise with which Sister Abigail heard this confession.

The man went on excitedly, saying, "I have two pals. When we steal a purse we quickly empty the contents into our pockets, and throw the purse away. When we get home at night, we put the day's haul together and divide it up. When I took out the contents of your purse, instead of opening a folded bill, I found this paper." Taking out the little card upon which Sister Abigail had written her address. "See what I read: 'Whosoever' (in bright red ink)—that means you— *'For God so loved the world that He gave His only begotten Son that whosoever believeth in Him should not perish but have everlasting life.'* It shot like a bolt of lightning through my mind, but turning it over I saw that…" Holding up the card, she saw "Whosoever (in blazing red) that means you— *'Whosoever was not found written in the Book of Life was cast into the lake of fire.'"*

"Well," he continued, "I was in hell all night last night. I thought that card would burn a hole in my hand. I can't get away from that word; it's God speaking to me. I've come to confess to you, and let you call the police and give me up.

"Give you up to the police?" questioned Sister Abigail.

"Yes. I'm a thief and a robber. I've made my living stealing, and I've robbed you."

"No," said Sister Abigail. "I can't do that. God has spoken to you." Taking up her Bible and opening at the eighth chapter of the Gospel of John, she read:

And the scribes and Pharisees brought unto Him a woman taken in adultery; and when they had set her in the midst, they say unto Him, Master, this woman was taken in adultery, in the very act. Now, Moses in the law commanded us that such should be stoned: but what sayest Thou? This they said, tempting Him, that they might have to accuse Him. But Jesus stooped down, and with His finger wrote on the ground, as though He heard them not. So when they continued asking Him, He lifted up Himself, and said unto them, He that is without sin among you, let him first cast a stone

PROVIDER & PROTECTOR

at her. And again he stooped down, and wrote on the ground. And they which heard it being convicted by their own conscience, went out one by one, beginning at the eldest, even unto the last: and Jesus was left alone, and the woman standing in the midst. When Jesus had lifted Himself up, and saw none but the woman, He said unto her, Woman, where are those thine accusers? hath no man condemned thee? She said, No man, Lord. And Jesus said unto her, Neither do I condemn thee: go, and sin no more" (Jn. 8:3-11).

Laying down the Bible, Sister Abigail asked, "Do you think I could condemn you, or give you up to the law? I too, am a sinner, and there is only this difference between us: I am a sinner saved by the blood of Jesus Christ, and you also will one day be saved by His grace through His sacrifice on the cross of Calvary."

"Did He do all this for me? Did He die for me?" he cried.

"Yes, for you," and there in that little room, this thief received the Lord Jesus Christ as his Saviour.

The man then told his life-story. He was the only child of Christian parents. His father died when he was very young. A guest visiting his home when he was a little boy had taught him sleight-of-hand tricks. He became quite expert in taking things from people's pockets and then would ask the person for the article. He greatly enjoyed seeing the person's surprise at finding the article gone. He then taught two of his little boy friends these tricks,

GOD IS FAITHFUL

and it so fascinated these children that at ten years of age, with these two playmates, he ran away from home. For many years they had made their living as pickpockets. He had seen his mother a very few times during those years, but we know her prayers had followed him.

He told Sister Abigail, that on the night when he attacked her four years previous, when she began to say "Whosoever," it brought his mother before him, for she used to teach him that text. It angered him so that he wanted to kill her when he threw her into the snowbank. But God was watching our sister. Not only that, a mother's prayers for her wayward son were yet to be answered—and Sister Abigail was the instrument which God would use for this purpose.

The story being told, the man said that he must hurry away to tell his two friends about Him, and then leave them, to find work and live an honest life.

Returning to his friends, he told them as best he could the story of the cross and how his sins had been put away by the blood of Christ. "Well," said they, "you taught us to serve the devil and brought us into this life. If it isn't good enough for you, it isn't good enough for us."

He brought the two friends to Sister Abigail and she told them of God's love for sinners, and that Christ died for them too, and they both received Him as their Saviour. *"As many as received Him to them gave He power to become the Sons of God, even to them that believe on His name"* (Jn. 1:12)

They were anxious to know what to do with the money which they had in the bank, about three hundred dollars, as they could not return it to the owners. She advised them to use it in helping other young men whom they might seek to bring to Christ.

Leaving the city and its temptations, "Jacob and his brethren," as Sister Abigail lovingly called them, went to the country. For a number of years at odd times she heard from them. They were all working and earning an honest living, and all were soul-winners.

In April of 1918, Sister Abigail received a phone call asking her to come to the train station and meet some soldiers enroute for France. To her joy she found the khaki-clad men were her friends, "Jacob and his brethren." They had enlisted as ambulance drivers, and although at that time were above the draft age, had enlisted solely to be soldiers of the cross.

The weaving of the pattern is not yet finished. God alone knows the design, but He permitted Sister Abigail to see a little of His wonder working for "Little is much when God is in it!" She tells the story in her own words:

THE SEQUEL TO THE STORY

About six years ago as I was traveling from Hamilton,

GOD IS FAITHFUL

Ontario to Buffalo, a gentleman, a lady and a little child sat near me on the train. I noticed that the gentleman had lost one arm and one leg, no doubt in the late war. Noticing that the little child was restless and the mother looked weary, I offered to relieve her of her burden for a short time. Taking out of my bag a round celluloid mirror with a text, *"For God so loved the world, that He gave His only begotten Son, that whosoever believeth in Him should not perish, but have everlasting life"* (John 3:16) printed on the back. I gave it to the child to amuse her.

After a while, the baby dropped it and the mother picked it up. Carefully examining it, she said to her husband, "Why, George, this is just like the one the man gave to you in France!" Having it in his pocket, he took it out to compare it with this one to see if it were the same.

After a few moments of silence, he said, turning to me, "Is your name Love?"

"No," I answered, "but my name is Luffe."

Again a silence.

The man said "Pardon me, Madam, but I have been shell-shocked and my memory is not very good. Madam, do you live in Buffalo?"

"Yes," I replied.

Then waiting again to collect his thoughts, he asked, "Did you ever know a man by the name of Jacob?"

I said, "Yes."

PROVIDER & PROTECTOR

Then again silence.

He then said, "Mrs. Luffe, he saved me in France, and hundreds of others. He would go down into the trenches where the men were wounded and dying and whisper into their ears the gospel of Jesus Christ, that if they believed that God so loved the world that He gave His only begotten Son to die on the cross of Calvary for them they would go to heaven. One man said, 'I have paid the supreme sacrifice.' He told him that there was only one 'supreme sacrifice.' That was the death of Jesus Christ the Son of God upon the cross of Calvary. Believing this he would be saved. Ever after that he told each one to whom he spoke that the only supreme sacrifice was the death of Jesus Christ on the cross of Calvary.

"One day he was struck in the arm by a passing shell. Physicians made every effort to save his life but he died serving his country and his God."

What a remarkable instance that I should have learned of the last days of that "holdup" man, a pickpocket who became a winner of souls for the Christ who saved him!

Clara S. Feilder, *Sister Abigail,* Grand Rapids, MI: Gospel Folio Press, 1937, pp. 169-176; 187-197.

EIGHTEEN

All Along the Way

Andrew Stenhouse was introduced to the Lord's work in South America during his travels as a radio officer in the Merchant Marine. He was especially impressed with the need in Argentina and soon realized the Lord was calling him there as a missionary. He and his wife Nina served in Argentina for two years until the Lord led them to Chile where they labored for Him for more than fifty years.

As soon as our wedding ceremony had been performed, application was made to Ottawa, Canada for a passport in my wife's name, and it was reckoned that within a month's time we should be on our way to the southern hemisphere. We began to make arrangements accordingly, and reservations were made on passages from Halifax to New York on a ship due to sail on the Saturday of Easter week. But the date drew near, and the passport had not arrived. We urgently requested that it be sent without delay to an address in Halifax, and we ourselves proceeded there to await its arrival.

We only got possession of it on Good Friday, the day before the ship's departure, and on that day it was not possible to get the necessary visa from the Argentine vice-consul. The ship was due to sail at eight o'clock on Saturday morning, and the office of the Consulate would not open until nine. There was nothing we could do but pray, and God graciously answered our petition, for the ship's sailing was delayed until midday, which gave us ample time to attend to our business.

This may appear to be a small matter, but in the light of subsequent events it was quite important. In itself it was an indication, the first of many, that God was willing to intervene in our affairs with *"well-timed help, coming just when we needed it"* (see Heb. 4:16, AMP.). But it was more than that, for it was the first link in a whole chain of events, and on it depended all the rest. God knew that it was necessary that we should sail from Halifax on that very day, and He arranged accordingly.

The American transit visa which we had obtained permitted us to remain in New York for a couple of weeks—just long enough for us to make the connection with a ship proceeding to the Argentine. We accordingly made reservation on that ship by depositing a certain proportion of the fare, trusting God to supply the remainder before the sailing date. At no time, and to no one, did we give the slightest hint that there was any lack in that respect. It was a principle with us that our needs would be made known to God alone.

Again the "well-timed help" was provided in ways that we could not have foreseen, and 24 hours before our ship was due to sail the balance of our fare was paid. Moreover, through the kindness of Christian friends in the clothing business, we were equipped with lightweight clothing suitable for the Argentine climate; and for this we were more than thankful. We also had a balance of fourteen dollars in our pocket with which to disembark in South America! Fourteen dollars and the Lord God Almighty were quite enough.

GOD GOES BEFORE

In due time our ship docked in Buenos Aires, and we were met and welcomed by several of the missionaries whom we had advised of our expected arrival. We had not formulated any plans as to where we might go or what we might do while "marking time" in the Argentine, nor did we reveal to anyone that our thought was to eventually cross the Andes Mountains into Chile. If this was the Lord's mind for us, He would confirm it; and in the meantime we would wait on Him for guidance.

Mr. and Mrs. Sam Williams kindly received us into

GOD IS FAITHFUL

their home for a few days while we visited some of the friends with whom I had previously had contact. Among these friends were Mr. and Mrs. Enoch Brown, in the neighboring suburb of Avellaneda. When asked by them what we intended doing, we simply replied that we were looking to the Lord for guidance as to that. This evoked from them the question, "Have you seen the Lawries yet?" I replied that we hoped to do so soon. Mr. Brown suggested that we endeavor to see them as soon as possible, but without giving us any reason. We decided, however, that he must have had some special reason in mind, and agreed to visit these friends on the following day.

Mr. Brown, however, did some more thinking and praying about the matter, and the Lord laid it on his heart to rise very early next morning and cross a considerable section of the city in order to intercept Mr. Lawrie before he left his home to go to business. The result was that an arrangement was made for us to meet with the said brother that day at the lunch hour in the heart of Buenos Aires. How very much depended on that!

I had met Mr. Lawrie and his good wife a few years previously, but the acquaintance was only slight, and we had not exchanged any correspondence. What we learned in that lunch hour conversation was this: (a) that brother Lawrie and his wife were contemplating a six-month's absence from the country in order to visit their native

ALL ALONG THE WAY

Scotland and that they were ready to leave in about a week's time: (b) that they needed a Christian couple to occupy their home during those six months and at the same time take an interest in the little Gospel Hall that they had built alongside their house; and (c) that they had been praying for months that God would supply such a couple and were still waiting for the answer to their prayers. And then came the proposition: Would we consider occupying the house rent free for that time?

Not much consideration was necessary to arrive at the conclusion that this was the Lord's doing and another example of the "well-timed help" that we had already begun to experience. Just how well-timed it was came to light more clearly when we talked things over in the Lawrie's home that evening. We had been invited to see the place before giving a definite answer, and when we finally said "Yes," brother Lawrie showed quite a bit of emotion; and then he explained why.

It seems that the Lawries had not heard that we were on our way to the Argentine, and they had no idea as to how the Lord might answer their prayers. We were not in their thoughts at all, and it seemed to them as though no answer was forthcoming. And so it was that when their sailing date lay just one week ahead, they felt obliged to do something else. What they did was to put an advertisement in an English-language newspaper offering the house on special terms for a six-month period. That advertisement had already appeared on or before the day of our conversation with Mr. Brown; and this was the reason for his early-morning visit to the Lawries. Had he not gone there, brother Lawrie from his office would have answered one of the letters received from the various applicants; but as it was, the letters were still in his pocket unanswered, and the house was still available for us. Was it just a coincidence that the contact was made just an hour or two before it would have been too late?

As we reflected on God's well-timed arrangements, we realized more definitely why it was that He had not permitted any delay in our sailing from Halifax that Saturday morning about a month before, and we were more than ever encouraged to look to Him for guidance and allow Him to have the control of all our movements.

Mr. and Mrs. Lawrie were exceedingly kind to us and left a well-stocked pantry when the time came for their departure. Our occupation of their home for a period of six months meant that we could give ourselves without distraction to the study of the language, and the meetings in the little hall alongside provided opportunity for practice. Mr. Brown came along weekly for ministry meetings, and Mr. Lester, a business brother, was also a frequent visitor. The latter was a helpful critic when the time came for me to begin taking part in the meetings.

A HOME ON WHEELS

It had come to our notice meantime that there existed in the country a motor Bible coach, that is, a vehicle intended to be used as living quarters while its occupants engaged in the work of selling the Scriptures and distributing gospel literature in the country districts. It had formerly been used for a period of about seven years, but recently it had been in disuse for about five years, and nobody seemed to be particularly interested in using it for the purpose for which it was intended. From the time we heard of it, the idea of getting it out of its garage and on the roads again appealed to us. As we were not interested in taking up permanent residence in the Argentine, we were more free for that kind of itinerary work.

So it was that when Mr. and Mrs. Lawrie returned from Scotland, and we had spent one more month occupying the home of Mr. and Mrs. Brown in Avellaneda in order to free them for a vacation in Uruguay, we were ready to take to the road. Mr. Nicholas Doorn, who had more experience with the coach than anyone, offered to accompany us north as far as his hometown of Bell-Ville, and it was agreed that we would make that town our base for a time.

The Bible coach was quite a vehicle. It was a Model-T Ford, with a body built to order. At the time of which I speak it was about twelve years old and had been used and abused in a variety of ways. In its interior was a divan-type seat, the back of which could be hooked up into a horizontal position, thus providing, theoretically, two sleeping-berths—upper and lower. The leather upholstery, however, had become somewhat worn, and the springs tended to protrude in places—not always the best places to correspond to our anatomy! In one corner was a small cookstove, and in another, a collapsible wash basin. There was a miniature wardrobe (the designer had Matthew 10:10 in mind), a folding table, and several cupboards for Bibles and gospel literature, and that was about all. Outside there was a platform which could be pulled out from underneath the chassis and hooked up into position for open-air preaching. This was the vehicle which was to serve us as our living-quarters (about six feet by nine) during much of the time that we were to remain in the Argentine, which proved to be about two more years.

A CHAPTER OF MIRACLES

About this time there was a big change in the weather. It became very cold and the roads became hard with the frost. We remember particularly one cold morning when we awoke to find that a jug of drinking water in the interior of the coach had a coat of ice on the top of it. But the hard roads, we thought, would be better than the soft muddy ones, so we set off with the thought of being at the town of Alta Gracia (in the direction of Cordoba) for the occasion of a big national holiday which lay ahead.

But we had not proceeded far when our troubles began afresh. First one tire, and then another, gave way, and there was no place anywhere near where we could have them vulcanized. I decided it would be necessary to remove both of the back tires and crawl on the rims of the wheels to the nearest village. But in the process of jacking up the back axle, the jack suddenly collapsed and refused to function anymore. So we then decided that we had come to a full stop, and not just a semi-colon.

I thought of the possibility of putting a block of wood under the axle and digging under the wheels in order to remove the tires, but the ground was very hard and my sturdy little spade (a faithful friend on many previous occasions) made little impression. My good wife sat in the front seat of the vehicle and prayed. I asked her what she thought of this situation, and she said, "It must be Romans 8:28, but I don't just see it right now." We asked ourselves what would God do now.

After a while a vehicle appeared in the distance. It was a truck from the city of Cordoba, and presently it drew up and came to a standstill. The first thing the driver did was to produce some fruit and offer it to my wife; and after this friendly gesture he informed us that he was a believer. He had not yet been baptized, but he had been attending meetings of an assembly in Cordoba and had been converted a short time before. Moreover, he had heard about the wonderful Bible coach and was able to recognize it immediately. What could he do for us?

It did not take long to explain our predicament, and he knew immediately what had to be done. Producing a jack, he soon had the tires removed, and he took charge of these, along with a spare which also needed repairing. "Now," he said, "there is a little hamlet just two kilometers ahead of you. You will have to drive there slowly, but I will go ahead of you and arrange with the owner of a little country inn to receive the coach in custody for a few days. Then you will take the train for Cordoba, taking the tires along with you to have them vulcanized." Then, looking at his watch, he said, "But you have no time to lose; the train will arrive at ten minutes to seven, and if you lose it, there will be no other until Monday at the same time." (This was Saturday evening about 6:20.)

Leaving two tracks on the road behind us, we got to the place where our Good Samaritan friend was waiting for us, and the coach was duly installed in the interior court of the inn. I was still in overalls looking very grimy, and in the few moments available I had to wash and change and pack a small suitcase with the aid of a paraffin lamp, for darkness had now come down. The lamp presently sputtered and went out, and the operation was finished more by faith than by sight.

We lost no time and rushed to the railway station. The train was already there, and our friend was holding it. He had put the tires in the luggage van, and as we arrived he handed us our tickets and bade us Godspeed. He paid all expenses, and was happy to do it; which was all to the good, for we had very little money.

As we settled down for the two-hour journey to Cordoba, we marvelled at the Lord's doings and reflected that "Omnipotence hath servants everywhere." The place where our breakdown occurred was a desolate part of the country, with very little vehicular traffic on the road, and our new-found friend told us that he hardly ever had occasion to travel that way. Yet he had arrived that day at the appointed place, and at the appointed time, with no minutes to spare.

THE DRAMA CONTINUES

Now we were on our way to Cordoba earlier than we had expected, and what would we do on arrival there? It was the weekend of a big national holiday (July 9). On that date there was to be a conference at Tucuman (much further north) and we had understood that brethren Clifford and Russell (residents of Cordoba) both intended being present at that conference. We had no other addresses than theirs in Cordoba, so where would we go? We had no money to go to a hotel (the reason for this constant scarcity of funds will come to light later), but we had experienced enough of the lovingkindness of our God to trust Him to take care of any future emergencies.

We got to Cordoba about nine o'clock that Saturday night, and after depositing the three tires at the station, we stepped out onto the street. The Cliffords, we had been informed, lived alongside the Gospel Hall on Boulevard Guzman, not far from the railway station; so our first thought was to go there and ascertain whether any of the Clifford family were at home.

There was no response to our ringing of the bell, but when we knocked on the gate, someone emerged from a house alongside and informed us that the whole family had gone away and would be absent for several days.

And now what? We retraced our steps in the direction of the station and paused on a corner to ask for guidance. On the street at which we had arrived tram cars were passing frequently, and presently one arrived with the inscription "San Vicente." That seemed to ring a bell in our memory, and then we recalled that the Arab brother who accompanied Mr. Clifford and Mr. Russell to Rio Tercero had told us that he lived in San Vicente. His name was Hani, but we did not have his address, and San Vicente was a large suburban area of Cordoba. To look

ALL ALONG THE WAY

for a man called Hani in that area at about ten o'clock at night would be like looking for the proverbial needle in a haystack. So why go to San Vicente? It did not seem reasonable.

We allowed that tram car to pass, but as we waited, we got the impression that we should take the next one going in that direction and see what happened. After all, God did not bring us to Cordoba in a providential manner in order to leave us stranded on a street corner. So when the next car for San Vicente came along, we boarded it.

It was fairly full, but as we looked down the aisle we spied a couple of seats and proceeded to occupy them, my wife on one side and I on the other. What was my surprise then to discover that I was sitting alongside Mr. Hani—the brother we wanted to find!

Brother Hani was as surprised to see us as we him. He gave us a warm welcome to his home, and when we told our story of the day's events, he wept. Then he told us his story.

He had been to town and was in the act of boarding a tram car to return home when suddenly he remembered about buying something to take home with him; so he popped into a nearby shop and was out again before the next car arrived. The car he got down from was the one we allowed to pass, and the car he got into was the one we boarded at the next stop.

GOD IS FAITHFUL

But there was more to tell. The Hanis' house was small; just a living-room and bedroom, and they never had been able to entertain visitors. But just a short time before our arrival, brother Hani had become exercised about this. As an elder in the assembly, he knew that he ought to show hospitality, and this is what he wanted to do. So he got busy and had a small room erected in a corner of the back yard, and that room, he told us with glee, was only just ready for occupation; the paint was just dry. He told us to make ourselves at home, and we were glad to do so.

Next day (the Lord's Day) he announced to the assembly the reason for our unexpected arrival in Cordoba, and exhorted the Christians with regard to their responsibility in connection with the Bible coach work. He also got in touch with another assembly about the same matter, and as a result two new tires were provided for the coach. Of the three old ones, two were discarded and the other was vulcanized.

Before we left San Vicente to return to the abandoned vehicle, Brother Hani gave us a warm invitation to return soon and make full use of the prophet's chamber for as long as we might want to use it as our base of operations in the Cordoba area. For this invitation we could not be too thankful, and this for a very special reason, which I will now proceed to explain.

REDIRECTED MAIL

For some time we had been conscious of an almost complete lack of correspondence from the homelands, and we could not even guess at the reason for it. We did not know why our brook should have dried up so completely. But about the time of our arrival in Cordoba the truth came to light. Our correspondence from abroad went to the post office box of Mr. Enoch Brown in Buenos Aires and was forwarded by him to the various addresses that we supplied to him from time to time. But there came a time when the postal authorities in Buenos Aires made a new regulation to the effect that the post office boxes could only be used by the people who rented them. And so it was that letters addressed to "care of such-and-such a box" were weeded out and returned to the senders. The result of this was that for a period of months we received practically no mail at all.

In these circumstances it was necessary to provide the friends at home with a new address, so that the returned letters might be forwarded to us. In those days no one thought of air mail, so letters from Britain or the U.S. took about a month to come; and those that had been returned to the senders actually took three months to get back to us. We therefore had need of patience and confidence in the God of Elijah.

Instead of a widow woman, God had provided for us

this worthy couple who gave us unstinted hospitality. Because of the special circumstances of our encounter that Saturday night, brother Hani was convinced that God had sent us to his home that he might assume responsibility for our welfare.

Andrew Stenhouse, *Counting on God,* Waynesboro, GA: Christian Missions Press, 1976, pp. 12-16; 33-37.

NINETEEN

Hitchhiking on Purpose

When George Watmaugh got saved, he had a great desire to tell others about the Lord. He began hitchhiking back and forth across America, looking for occasions to share the gospel—a ministry that lasted more than thirty years and gave him many opportunities to testify to the faithfulness of God.

For the past thirty years I have been doing what the Holy Spirit told Philip to do: *"Go near, and join thyself to this chariot"* (Acts 8:29). And the Lord has kept me all these fifty-four trips across America from ever being hurt in an accident or late for a meeting, for which I praise His Name.

I was raised in a home where I can never recall seeing a Bible or hearing a word of prayer. My father was a hard drinker and my only brother committed suicide. I got off to a bad start and wasted some of the best years of my life in professional boxing. Then I became interested in show business. I was in an act with two comedians in Stamford, Connecticut, which wasn't going very well. But in those days Hollywood was the land of opportunity, so I packed all my belongings into two suitcases, shipped them from New York to Hollywood, and hopped a freighter to try to sell our act out there.

I arrived all right, but my suitcases never did—I haven't seen them to this day. They got lost—but I got saved!

I couldn't sell our act in Hollywood—it was almost impossible for anyone unknown to get a break out there, but I managed to get work in two movies.

SAVED IN HOLLYWOOD

One night in 1933, I heard Paul Rader on the radio. He was having gospel meetings nearby; out of curiosity I went to hear him. For the first time in my life I saw that all my sin had been laid on Christ, who had made atonement for sin when He died upon the cross. Believing that Christ died as my substitute, I was justified, made as righteous as if I had never committed one act of sin! That was good news to me.

When the Lord found me, there were many things I didn't know, but one thing I was sure of: I was a new creation in Christ! My whole life had been transformed by His wonderful grace, and I had a great desire to tell others about Him. So I started hitchhiking, never dreaming I would be at it all these years.

It's so long ago that I can't remember the details of my early trips, except that I saw that hitchhiking was a good way to get close to men and tell them what the Lord had saved me from and to. As I rode along, the conviction grew that this was to be my service for the Lord, because it came easily and men would listen.

I had no home then, so I just lived out of a suitcase and kept going wherever the Lord led.

FROM HAND TO MOUTH

A few months after I left Los Angeles, I was in Wyoming, sheltering from a storm on the porch of a store. Feeling a little down in the dumps, I recalled what one of God's servants once said, "When you get down in the cellar of despondency, look around for the King's wine."

Just then a young man rolled up in his car and, since there was no hotel for miles, I asked him if I might sleep in his car for the night. He said he was working on a road job ten miles down the road and if I would come along to the camp, I could sleep in his car.

He happened to be a Mormon and we talked until after midnight. Some time that early morning I believe I led him to our Lord. Then he got me a blanket and in the morning he went over to the mess hall and arranged a good breakfast for me. It is wonderful to live from hand to mouth *when it's God's hand and my mouth.*

The next morning the very first car to come along gave me a ride to Cody, the place I tried to get to the day before. Surely the steps and the stops of a good man are ordered by the Lord.

WHERE HE LEADS HE FEEDS

Shortly after I was converted I found myself walking along Hope Street in Los Angeles without a penny in my pocket and a little discouraged. As I passed the cafeteria of the Bible Institute of Los Angeles, the thought came to me, "If these people knew how hungry I was, surely they would let me work for a meal," but I felt so weak I didn't feel I could talk to anyone. I said to myself, "I'll just go in and order a meal and then tell the manager my predicament and offer to work the rest of the day or longer for the meal.

While I was eating, a fine looking man came over and sat at my table and introduced himself as Dr. Arthur I. Brown. We had a nice time of fellowship and, without his knowing that I was financially embarrassed, he reached over and picked up my check, saying, "Let me pay this," and shaking my hand, off he went. The Lord said to Elijah, *"I have commanded the ravens to feed thee there."*

HITCHHIKING ON PURPOSE

The ravens knew where "there" was, and if you are "there" you'll get fed. Where He leads He feeds.

I recall hearing a story of a young Bible student standing in front of this same cafeteria, reading the menu for the day posted on the door. A returned missionary was standing alongside him, reading it also. The young student blurted out, "Can you beat it, dried beef on toast again today!"

The missionary took hold of his arm and said, "Young man, don't you ever sing, 'Where He leads me I will follow,' until you have learned to say, 'What He feeds me I will swallow.'"

How wonderfully the Lord has supplied my every need for more than thirty years without my ever knowing for sure where a dollar would come from. "Great is Thy faithfulness, Oh God, my Father!"

I have often said jokingly, "I have never missed a meal, just postponed a few." There have been days when I have missed a meal simply because a place to eat could not be found. There was one of these days while I was crossing Louisiana. I had an early breakfast and now it was five in the afternoon. I was getting very hungry, when a young soldier stopped to give me a ride. One of the first things he said, after getting acquainted, was, "If you get hungry there is a bag on the back seat full of fried chicken my mother fixed, so just help yourself."

THE PROBLEM SOLVER

Leaving Buffalo one morning, a man in a nice Packard stopped to give me a ride. As I witnessed to him, he stopped me by saying, "Mister, you're talking to the most defeated and discouraged man that ever picked you up. I feel like running this car into a pole." Then he told me some of his troubles. He had buried his dear wife that year, then his home had burned to the ground, and then he lost his business—six trucks and a steam shovel. How glad I was we could pull to the side of the road and tell him of a Saviour that

> *...can solve every problem,*
> *The tangles of life can undo.*
> *There is nothing too hard for Jesus*
> *Nothing that He cannot do.*

FIVE VERSES FOR A BROKEN HEART

Not far out of St. Louis, early one morning, I was picked up by a young man, six-foot-six, red-headed and freckled face, if you can feature that. He was one of the most likeable men I have ever met.

After I witnessed to him for some time, he said, "I was in the Marines in this last war and in two major battles but right this morning I am going through the worst battle in my life. I've just said goodbye to my wife. I love her more than anything in the world but for more than a year she has been unfaithful. I've tried everything, but this morning I gave up and handed her some keys and said, 'Here, you can have all I've got. I'm getting in that car out there and I'm going to start riding.' Now I picked you up."

"Well, this didn't happen by accident. Before I left my room this morning, I asked the Lord to get me a ride with someone who needs help that only God can give." Taking out my New Testament I said, "There are five wonderful verses in this Book. They were a great blessing to me years ago and I believe they can be a help to you. I want you to read them."

We went down the road a few miles before he turned to me and said, "If I pull over there, will you show me those verses now?"

"Indeed I will!" I replied. So he pulled over to the side of the road.

"The first one is John 5:24." I found the place and handed him the Book, and he read: *"Verily, verily, I say unto you, He that heareth My word, and believeth on Him that sent Me, hath everlasting life, and shall not come into condemnation; but is passed from death unto life."*

The next one was John 1:12: *"But as many as received Him, to them gave He power to become the sons of God, even to them that believe on His name."*

And of course there was John 3:16: *"For God so loved the world, that He gave His only begotten Son, that*

GOD IS FAITHFUL

whosoever believeth in Him should not perish, but have everlasting life."

Ephesians 2:8 followed: *"For by grace are ye saved through faith; and that not of yourselves: it is the gift of God: not of works, lest any man should boast."*

Finally, he read Romans 10:9-10: *"If thou shalt confess with thy mouth the Lord Jesus, and shalt believe in thine heart that God hath raised Him from the dead, thou shalt be saved. For with the heart man believeth unto righteousness; and with the mouth confession is made unto salvation."*

After those five verses, I had him read quite a few more. After some time, the young man trusted Christ as His Saviour, and was taken out of bondage into glorious liberty. After we both prayed, he took me by the hand, and we agreed that he was going to call his wife and tell her what had happened.

"May this be the means of bringing our home together," said the young man. It is wonderful what God can do with a broken heart when He has all the parts.

About a week later, I was given a ride with a young sailor, who was on his way back to Seattle after spending a short leave with his wife and month-old baby. We talked about eternal things for a long time. As I was driving his car, I handed him my New Testament and asked him to read out loud those same five verses. After he read the last verse I referred to, he kept right on reading for the next fifty miles. Before we reached Denver, I pulled to the side of the road and he trusted the One who had died in his place as his Saviour.

You will never know the heartaches that are running up and down the highways until you get seated alongside some of these men. I believe the best place in all the world to talk to a man is beside him in his car. He can't go to sleep and he can't go away.

Always remember an argument may close the man's mouth, but it takes the gospel to open his heart. The gospel is not good advice—quit this and do something else—but "good news." The good news is, *"How that Christ died for our sins according to the Scriptures; and that He was buried, and that He rose again the third day according to the Scriptures"* (1 Cor. 15:3).

George Watmough, *Hitchhiking on Purpose,* Neptune, NJ: Loizeaux, 1965, pp. 9-16.

TWENTY

God is in the Details

Harry Brown and his wife, Margaret, left England in 1923 to serve the Lord in central Africa. These were primitive days, with no roads, railways, or any vehicles. For more than sixty years, the Browns labored in the gospel, medical work, and establishing assemblies. Harry also wrote a number of books of ministry in the African languages and recorded a great deal of ministry on tape.

A guide met us the day before we were to arrive at Luanza in the heart of Africa. He had been sent by Dan Crawford* to lead us a roundabout way to the top of the

---

* Dan Crawford, born in Scotland in 1870, was preparing for missionary work in China when he met F. S. Arnot in the autumn of 1888, the man on whom David Livingstone's mantle had fallen. Arnot won him to the need in Africa, and in 1889 he began blazing a trail for God through the Dark Continent until his death in 1926. His African name, Kongavantu, means "Gatherer of the People."

hill overlooking Luanza village. There we found Dan Crawford waiting for us with crowds of folk to give us a royal welcome; the noise was terrific. Dan came forward and gave us a welcome in English and in KiSwahili, the pure KiSwahili which I knew well. Then hundreds of folk began to sing hymns as we made our way to the brow of the hill.

We found ourselves looking down on a shelf upon which was set out the large village of Luanza, the streets running at right angles to each other and lined with avenues of shade trees, the houses looked very substantial. On the far edge of the shelf were the houses of the missionaries, and stretching out beyond these was a great lake, the farther side being invisible; this was Lake Mwerumukatamubundanshe. Sorry! I think I had better break it up for you: it is Mweru-mukata-mubunda-nshe. But I am sure you are none the wiser, so I will tell you what it means: "The great lake that drowns the locusts."

We stood there for a time admiring the wonderful view, then suddenly we were caught in a thunderstorm that blotted out the view and we had to dash for shelter in some nearby huts on the hill.

A REMARKABLE COUPLE

Our first meeting with Dan Crawford will ever be remembered. We found him to be a most remarkable per-

GOD IS IN THE DETAILS

son. He was medium height, fairly thick-set, had short crew-cut graying hair, a neatly trimmed pointed beard, and was wearing plus-fours and a light summer jacket. But it was his eyes that held our attention. They were light blue, sharp, and piercing, but there was quite a twinkle in them, and he certainly had a keen sense of humor; and all the time he was rattling off his remarks in English and KiSwahili, to him the one language was as easy as the other. He learned KiSwahili from the Arabs whom he often encountered in their ivory trading—white and black. And he had an old Arab who was proud to be the captain of the boat that had been sent out to Dan Crawford from Gourock in Scotland. It came out in two pieces and was then fitted together. The old Arab whose name was Jumaa, had fitted the boat with a latten sail, that is, a triangular sail extended by a long yard pole, a pole fastened at an angle to the mast.

When the storm was over, we began to descend the hill which was more of a cliff and very steep; reaching the bottom we passed along the streets until we came to the entrance to an avenue of palm trees leading up to Dan Crawford's house. The entrance was typically African, it was a framework of poles overlaid with strips of bright yellow reeds interwoven with strips of bark-rope dyed black, forming a pattern.

We walked through the avenue of palm trees and the

house came into view; a large squat building with a great thatched roof. We descended a few steps and came to a small quadrangle, paved with large flagstones from the surrounding hillside, and enclosed with a low framework covered with the same reed and bark-rope pattern. The verandah poles of the house were also framed like arches and the same light yellow reed and black bark-rope pattern, the spaces in the arches being filled in with reed work. It all looked most suitable in such a setting because it was African in material and design.

Mrs. Crawford was waiting for us and gave us a great welcome; we were soon convinced that she also was a remarkable person, and reckoned she would need to be if she was to keep up with a busy Dan Crawford. The more we saw of Dan Crawford the more we were convinced that there surely was only one tribe of Dan!

JUST A COINCIDENCE?

A few days after our arrival, Dan Crawford asked me if I knew anything about printing and printing machines. I told him I did not really know anything about either, but went on to tell him that when I was in Bristol at one time, a friend of mine took me through the printing works where he was manager, and that while he was doing so he pointed out to me a very old manually operated printing machine that they still used for odd jobs.

GOD IS IN THE DETAILS

I asked him if I could come in now and again to use it to print some of my leaflets advertising my tent meetings. He told me I was welcome to come and use it any time, and he would tell his foreman to show me how to set up the type and use the machine. It was not a power driven machine so there was no danger. I went in a few times and soon was able to manage the machine and produce some nice clean leaflets; it was a very old machine called an Albion.

Dan did a bit of a Highland Fling, then grabbed me by my arm and led me to a building attached to the place where the church met. He opened the door, pulled me inside and pointed to a printing press. I could hardly the believe my eyes—it was one of the old Albion presses, exactly like the one I had operated in Bristol.

Dan then told me that all the hymnbooks were falling to pieces and they were desperately needing a new edition printed. He asked me if I could possibly manage the job. I had a good look at the press and saw that it needed quite a bit of attention. It had never been properly set up. After a few days I had it all in good working order and started working on the hymnbooks. There were many trays of type, plenty of bits and pieces used in printing, also a stapling machine and a guillotine. When I handed over the first hundred copies of the hymnbook, Dan did a bit more of the Highland Fling.

WHEN THE HOUSE BURNED DOWN

In the midst of our pioneer activity in Mpweto, disaster struck. "Mulilo" (Fire!). We dashed outside as saw the kitchen roof a mass of flames. There was a strong wind blowing. We had to act quickly, but how? We had only one bucket and the water was about a mile away.

All we could do was stand and watch. The wind got worse and lumps of burning grass were blown further afield onto some nearby huts, and from them onto the old school building and from that onto the village. In an hour's time, all these buildings were just blackened ruins.

The African Christians wanted to come along and help in the work of rebuilding. I sorted them out and some went into the bush to get roofing poles, others to cut reeds and grass. One man had become quite good at ripping through planks with a ripsaw but he had too much strength, and in forcing the ripsaw through the hard wood he broke about nine inches off the end of it. This was most unfortunate because the handsaw would hardly bite into the hard wood. We felt terribly frustrated.

Then a wonderful thing happened. Just before sailing for Africa, we were asked to visit an assembly in Hoylake, Cheshire. They wanted to meet us both, hear from us how the Lord had been leading us, and give us their blessing.

A few days later, I had a letter from a Christian brother living in Boston, Lincolnshire. The letter contained a very substantial gift towards our passage out to Africa. He said he was on holiday in Hoylake and was at the meeting the night we were there.

Then a short time after our arrival in Luanza, I had another letter from him, asking if there was anything we specially needed because he would like to supply it.

SMALL REQUESTS, LARGE ANSWERS

Well, there was one thing we really did need, but we didn't think it would be fair to ask him to supply it—a typewriter! Before coming out to Africa, an old brother in the assembly at home told me he had an old typewriter that did not work and no one seemed able to repair it; but he knew I was a handyman, and if I could repair it, then I could have it. I took it home and fiddled about with it for a couple of hours, and then I typed him a nice letter thanking him for it!

It was a quaint machine, made by some German firm and called a Blick or some such name. I did a lot of work on it but it was so badly worn and needed some spare parts which I did not think I would be able to obtain; so I really did need a good typewriter; but I decided not to take advantage of the brother in asking him to supply me with one.

Instead of that, I asked if he would kindly send me a ripsaw, a handsaw, three wood chisels and three mortise chisels. In sending for these I had been thinking ahead and felt sure that I would be called upon to do quite a lot of woodwork. And now, a few days after the ripsaw was broken, I got a letter from a trader down by the lake telling me that a barge propelled by eight paddlers had unexpectedly arrived, and among other things they had a rather heavy packing case addressed to me. Would I send some carriers to pick it up?

I sent four carriers for it, and when I saw them staggering along the path with it I wondered whatever could be inside. It was a very strongly built packing case and it took me quite a time to get it opened up. To my amazement it was packed with tools. Tools of every description. They must have cost a fortune. Inside there was an inventory of the tools and an illustrated catalog of tools bearing the name of the brother I had written to for a couple of saws and a few chisels! He was a tool merchant—but I never knew it!

As we both looked at the tools we were speechless and wide-eyed. When Margaret found her voice she said, "You'll be able to make some nice pieces of furniture with tools like those, won't you, Darling?"

J. H. Brown, *A Missionary in the Making: Autobiography of J. H. Brown,* Pinelands, South Africa: self-published, n.d., pp. 137-138, 140-141, 150-154.

TWENTY-ONE

How Good is the God We Adore

In 1920, T. E. Wilson of Belfast heard Fred Lane speak of the unreached tribes of north Angola and of the need for a pioneer. At 18, he offered himself to God for this work. After a few years of language study and assessment of the need, he married Elizabeth, an American missionary and the two settled in Quirima. There were no Christians in the area, and no trace of civilization. Within sixteen years of pioneering with the gospel, there were 22 places where a gospel testimony had been established. One of the first converts crawled 120 miles on his hands and knees to hear the gospel! In 1940, the Wilsons moved to Kapango, opening up many new preaching centers. They left Angola in 1961.

After ten months in Portugal, I felt that the time had come to leave for Africa. All my needs had been supplied and I did not owe anyone anything. One day in counting my money, I found that I had sufficient to buy a third-class ticket on a Portuguese ship bound for Angola.

GOD IS FAITHFUL

The cost was about $45.00 at the present rate of exchange. After buying the ticket I had a little left over to buy some necessary articles. I had a sailmaker make me a small canvas tent. Then I bought a collapsible cot bed. The last item was a case of one hundred tins of sardines. I had heard that the Africans' staple diet was corn meal mush, and I thought that the sardines would at least make it palatable!

The day before I left Portugal an incident happened that was a great encouragement. Some friends in Ireland sent me a post office money order for £24. On sailing day I took this to the post office and the clerk cashed it in Portuguese currency. At that time the currency was very unstable and the exchange had soared to 150 escudos to the pound. In normal times it had been five to the pound. They had only notes of small denomination in the post office and I received a large parcel of money for my £24. When I arrived at the ship, I was allotted to a large cabin under the forecastle in which ten men were to sleep. Two of these were *degredados* (criminals) going out to Africa to complete a sentence for crimes committed in Portugal. They were being escorted by two soldiers. The other five in the cabin were Portuguese peasants. When I saw my traveling companions, I began to feel anxious about my parcel of money which in the cramped quarters it was practically impossible to conceal.

In three days we reached Madeira. I went ashore with my money and explained my problem to the manager of the bank. He changed my money back into English currency, charging me a small discount.

On the fifteenth day out from Lisbon, we reached Luanda, the capital of Angola. I went ashore again and met an Irish Methodist missionary, Robert Shields. He was very kind and hospitable, gave me some valuable advice, and then asked if he could help me to exchange my money. He introduced me to a German trader who changed my £24 into Portuguese currency at the rate of 220 escudos to the pound! He too had notes of small denomination, and, by the time he finished counting, my little pile had increased about 40 per cent.

Nothing was further from my mind than gambling on the money market, but it so happened that on the day I landed, the exchange had soared to its peak and then started to go down. Shortly afterwards the currency was stabilized at 100 escudos to the pound and later at 80 where it remained for many years. In any case, God saw my need and I had sufficient to pay my way through customs at Lobito and for subsequent expenses on the journey upcountry.

BREAKING NEW GROUND

I have felt for many years that, in a pagan country like

Central Africa, it is an unwise policy to isolate converts to Christianity from their own people. In doing so, they are spared persecution, but they are brought into a hothouse environment where healthy development is retarded. It is not good for the foreigner either. He is liable to get an exaggerated idea of his own importance. Recent independence movements in practically every part of Africa have proved that the principle of the missionary's building up a work around himself was wrong from the beginning. Sooner or later there is bound to be a reaction. Experience has shown that when the African is encouraged to accept responsibility from the commencement of his Christian life, he develops more naturally, and the work is on a much more solid foundation.

One day Mr. Fred Lane suggested to me that there was a need at a mission station called Hualondo, and that I might be able to help out there. It had been started many years before by George Murrain, a missionary from British Guiana. Murrain had recently died after an operation in America, and the work was being carried on by a young Englishman and his wife, Mr. and Mrs. Lance Adcock. He was not too well and was thinking of going home on furlough, but did not want to go unless there was someone to care for the work at Hualondo. Consequently I went over there and settled in.

Adcock was very keen on educational work, was a disciplinarian, and a very clever linguist. He suggested that I help in the school, and while I had little liking or fitness for school teaching, I was glad of the opportunity for contact with the people. A Scripture lesson every day in Umbundu, which Adcock took, was a great help to me in learning the language. I lived at Hualondo for eighteen months. After the Adcocks went home to England, I was some months alone on the place. Here I made my first attempts at preaching in the Umbundu language.

An incident occurred here which was a great encouragement in showing God's loving care for material needs.

A BURGLAR STRIKES

I was living in an adobe brick guest room which had belonged to the Murrains. It had a clay floor covered with bamboo mats and a homemade bed in the middle of the room. On the wall were some pegs, and all the clothes I had in the world, except what I was wearing, were hanging on the pegs. In the corner was a homemade desk where I kept my money, papers, and correspondence.

One night, while I was out at the prayer meeting, an African burgled the place. He first tried to pry open the window with the blade of his ax, but I had secured it with screws from the inside and he failed to open it. He then tried the lock. He put a plug of tobacco against it to deaden the sound, and broke it with blows from his ax. He

GOD IS FAITHFUL

then went in and plundered the room. When I came back from the prayer meeting, I found the bed stripped and the clothes and the contents of the desk gone. I was practically left in the middle of Africa with the clothes I was standing up in.

The next day, the man who did it came and clucked with his tongue and sympathized with me in my loss. It was only two years later that I found out he was the culprit!

I felt pretty miserable. In those days it was not easy to get supplies in the country, but I tried to be as philosophical about it as I could.

A couple of weeks later, an African turned up with a large bundle on his head. It was sewn up in cloth and had been sent on from the railhead in Silva Porto. When I opened it, I found sheets, pillow cases, clothing, and underwear, and in the center a letter from some ladies in Belfast, Ireland. It contained money which they said was to defray customs on the parcel and they hoped the contents would prove useful. On examining the datestamp, I found it had been sent off a couple of months before the robbery happened. It had been beautifully timed, and here was everything duplicated and brand new!

BLACKWATER FEVER

After two years of work, following my marriage to

Elizabeth, our little mud-and-wattle home in the woods was finished and furnished with all handmade furniture. A crude meeting place had been built, school and medical work organized as well as regular meetings for preaching and teaching. A number of Chokwes had confessed Christ as Saviour, had been baptized, and the foundations of a New Testament church was laid.

During this time the Lord gave us our first child, a little boy. For the birth we decided to go down to Luma-Casai, where we had been married. This meant a ten days' walk in the wet season. Elizabeth had a hammock and bearers to help her over the hard places.

The worst experience was crossing the Kuhafu River, which was in flood. All the stick bridges had been carried away by the current. We camped on the river bank, while I went up and down the river, looking for a ford where we could cross without having to swim. I found a place where the water was up to the shoulders of the men at its deepest point. The African carriers suggested that Elizabeth lie down on the wooden framework of the awning of the hammock; then two men hoisted this on top of their heads, and, with two other men balancing the burden on either side, they walked across the river, with the water often up to their necks.

When we arrived at Luma-Casai, we found our old friend Dr. Jacobs was there as well as Susan MacRae, a

GOD IS FAITHFUL

very competent nurse from Framingham, Massachusetts. Our first child, David, was born April 1, 1928, in the home of Miss MacRae. There were complications and we were very thankful for the skill and care of the doctor and nurse who saved Elizabeth's life. If it had not been for their devoted help, she would have died.

When the baby was a few weeks old, we returned to our home at Chitutu.

The Lord later gave us two other children, Thomas Ernest in 1932, and Elizabeth Ann in 1935. While our children were growing up, we did not have a doctor or registered nurse within reach, and although they were exposed to all kinds of tropical disease and accident, we are thankful that they were preserved from serious illness and grew up strong and healthy.

When baby David was nine months old, Elizabeth came down with blackwater fever. We had made several itinerating journeys in the Luandu River region where there are many swamps and Anopheles mosquitoes. Both Elizabeth and I had been having recurrent attacks of malaria and in her case it ended in blackwater fever. This is a most serious and often fatal disease. The blood cells break down and are passed in the urine, which turns a dark brown, coffee color, which gives the disease its name. Many of the early missionaries died as a result of this malady.

HOW GOOD IS THE GOD WE ADORE

When this occurred it was the month of November, in the middle of the wet season. We were alone in the depths of the woods, our nearest missionary neighbors being the Bodalys at Chitau in Bié, six days' journey to the west. I wrote a letter to Mr. Bodaly, telling him what had happened, hoping that someone might be able to come to our help. I gave the letter to a Chokwe, called Mwachingongo, gave him a storm lantern so that he could travel after dark, and told him to get out to Chitau as quickly as he could. He could have done the journey in four days, traveling without a load, but, instead of hurrying, he loitered along the way and took about a week to get there. He told me afterwards that he thought the Ndona was going to die anyway and there was no use in hurrying!

In the meantime, I handed the baby over to a native girl to care for him, and I gave all my time and attention to Elizabeth. There was, of course, no medical help of any kind available, and while there was a government post about five miles away, the Portuguese officer in charge was absent, and in those days there was no radio communication or telephone contact with the outside.

At that time I had never seen a case of blackwater, although we have taken care of many since. For over a week I did not go to bed, but dozed and catnapped in a chair when I could. On the ninth day, Elizabeth had a relapse and I thought the end had come. On the thirteenth day she had a second relapse with uncontrollable hiccups, and again I gave up hope.

One day I heard what sounded like the hoot of an automobile horn, but thought I must have been dreaming and paid no attention. But then it sounded again. I went to the door and found two white men standing on the porch with the rain dripping off their clothes and a little automobile outside. It was Mr. Bodaly with his fellow worker, Edwin Roberts, an Englishman from London.

They had made an epochal journey from Chitau in the little auto under the most difficult conditions. There were two large rivers to cross, the Quanza and the Luandu, without bridges. Between the two rivers there was practically no road at all. The military, years before, had hacked a road through the virgin bush, but it was overgrown and covered with anthills and good-sized trees. When they came to the first river, the little car, an early compact called a Jowett, was lifted into two large dugout canoes, the two side wheels in each canoe tied together, and then paddled across. In the overgrown bush, an African rode on the running board, with an ax to chop down the trees which blocked the way. Again and again they had to be pushed and lifted out of swamps.

Their arrival was an indescribable relief and encouragement. Edwin Roberts was a comic. He described their incredible journey across the swamps in such a funny way that we laughed until our sides were sore. All our anxiety and troubles were forgotten.

Mr. Bodaly then told us that he must get back home the next day. But when we looked in the gas tank of the car it was nearly empty and the oil level was dangerously low. Needless to say there were no gas stations in the vicinity! But I had a good supply of kerosene which we burned in our lamps, and we filled up the tank with this. The Songo women had the custom of putting red mud and castor oil on their heads, so crude castor oil was easy to obtain. We filled up the sump of the car with this.

Next morning Mr. Bodaly had some difficulty getting the little auto to start, but finally he got it going. As far as I know he has never told the story of his return journey to Bié, burning kerosene and crude castor oil in the car, but he finally made it. Unfortunately it was the last journey that the longsuffering auto ever made! But we are most grateful to our good missionary friends and to the little car that gave its life to bring us help and comfort, and without a doubt saved my wife's life.

Mr. Roberts stayed with us and, after Mr. Bodaly had left, we had a serious talk about what we should do. Roberts had had considerable experience in medical work. He told us quite frankly that Elizabeth would not recover if we stayed where we were. We must get her out to Bié and send for competent medical help.

"But," I exclaimed, "how can we get her out in the middle of the wet season, in the rain, and across the flooded country between the Quanza and the Luandu Rivers?" Blackwater patients must lie flat on their back; if they attempt to sit up, there would be a relapse.

GOD OF THE WEATHER

"Let's pray about it," he replied. We asked God, if it was His will that we get out to Bié, that He would stop the rain for about a week until we arrived there. This seemed presumptuous when we considered the time of the year and the heavy rains which continued day after day. But we were up against it and had no alternative.

We sent for the local chief and told him what we planned to do. He promised to have men at the door the next morning to carry the hammock and the loads. When we awoke at dawn the rain had stopped, so we decided to start. A sailor's hammock slung from a palm pole, with a canvas awning over the top and sides, was prepared to carry the patient, and a smaller one to carry the baby. We put him in a basket, which was secured in the hammock with straps. Bed loads, food boxes, a tent in which to sleep at night, and odds and ends for the journey were hurriedly prepared and tied up.

The native porters carried the hammock into the bedroom, we wrapped Elizabeth in the blankets on the bed and carried her out. I quickly tidied up the place, turned the key in the door, and followed the men, the hammocks on ahead, the load men in single file, and Roberts and I bringing up the rear on foot. That day we pushed on until sundown. We covered over thirty miles and no rain had fallen. When we reached camp, we opened up a folding cot bed, lifted Elizabeth out of the hammock, and carried her into the tent. That night we had a praise meeting around the campfire. The Lord had answered our prayer for one day.

Next morning we were up early and on the path shortly after dawn. In the afternoon we ran into our first serious problem. The Luandu River, swollen with the heavy rains, was about 100 yards broad and a swift current was tearing at its banks. The river had both hippos and crocodiles. The only means of crossing was a frail dugout canoe which, when loaded with the paddler and a man with his load, was just about three or four inches above the surface of the water. When I looked at it my heart sank. But the paddler assured us that he could take the hammock with its burden safely across. He told us to fill the canoe half full of leaves, lay the hammock and patient on top and leave the rest to him!

I went up to the hammock, explained the situation to Elizabeth, and asked her what she thought about it. If she was nervous and would rather not attempt it, we would

GOD IS FAITHFUL

turn back to our home at Chitutu. She said she would rather go on, she would keep her eyes shut, and for us to get on with the job.

We carried the hammock down the bank, laid it in the bottom of the canoe, but held our breath when the paddler stepped in. The Songo paddlers stand up in the canoe and balance it with their two feet and the weight of their body. He did a magnificent job, paddling along the bank against the current upstream, then gently nosed the canoe diagonally with the current across the river and made a perfect landfall at the crossing. In the meantime I had stayed on the bank with a loaded and cocked gun, in case a croc or hippo should show its head. The hammock on the other side was lifted out and slung in the forks of two trees, while men and loads were ferried across. For the second day no rain had fallen, and we had another prayer and praise meeting that night around the campfire.

Our last hurdle was the Quanza, a much larger river than the Luandu but with much more sturdy dugouts for the crossing. A Portuguese trader called Sobral came down to the river with two Songo natives, who he said would take the hammock across. Instead of laying it in the bottom of the canoe, they proposed to stand up, with the ends of the palm pole on their shoulders, and the hammock swinging in midair. This seemed a nerve-racking experience for the patient, and again I asked her what she felt about it, and got the same reply as at the Luandu, "Let's get on with it." Men and loads were again safely transported to the other side.

Here Mr. Bodaly met us with a truck and soon we were at his home at Chitau. A guest room had been prepared with a comfortable bed and white sheets, which to us looked like a palace. We carried the patient in and then I went off with the men.

They were lined up on the verandah. While we were standing there talking, the great dark thunder clouds were gathering overhead, and before we had finished settling with the carriers, it had started to rain. We had been on the path for five days and not a drop of rain had fallen during the journey. Roberts and I looked at each other, but we couldn't speak. All we could think of was the little prayer meeting in the mud-and-wattle house at Chitutu when, in simple faith, we had asked the Lord to stop the rain until we got out to Bié. He had done just that!

That year we heard of four other cases of blackwater fever among white people in Angola. All four died; Elizabeth was the only one who recovered. (*Angola Beloved*, Neptune, NJ: Loizeaux, 1967, pp. 59-61, 77-79, 148-155.)

GOD'S SOVEREIGN WORK

The following interview was held with Mr. Wilson by his son, Tom, shortly before Mr. Wilson's homecall.

Q: Tell us about some of your early experiences.
A: I was saved on May 3, 1918, and two weeks later was baptized and received into the assembly at Donegal Road in Belfast. I was sixteen years of age at that time. In that same year I went to Harland and Wolf Shipyard and contracted for a five-year apprenticeship as a shipwright. But at the same time, during the five years I was in that apprenticeship, there was a Bible reading carried on by two men. Both of them belonged to area assemblies. For five years, every working day, I was at that Bible reading at lunch time.

At the same time I engaged in Sunday school work and open air gospel work. That was where I learned to preach. A group would go off to the villages around Belfast and have open air meetings.

Q: Did you have feelings then for the mission field?
A: A short time after I was saved, I committed my life to the Lord for full-time service. I was very interested in pioneer gospel work. As a young Christian I heard Fred Lane give an account of a journey just before coming home on furlough. He told about an unreached tribe in Angola and asked for prayer that someone might be raised up to go to that place. That was the first seed planted in my heart about going to Angola.

Q: What happened then?

HOW GOOD IS THE GOD WE ADORE

A: In October, 1923, I told the brethren of my exercise and shortly afterward they gave me a commendation to the work. I made preparations and booked passage to Portugal for language study. When I was getting on board ship to go to Portugal, Tommy Robinson was at the dock, bidding me goodbye. As he was shaking hands, he put two gold half sovereigns in my hand and said, "If you are ever down to your last penny, there is something to fall back on."

Q: What was a sovereign and what was it worth?

A: It was the equivalent of one English pound and was then worth five American dollars.

At that time, there were several books that made a deep impression on my life. One was the book on George Müller written by A.T. Pierson. I was impressed that he had never asked for money even though he had all those orphans dependent on him. I felt that I would like to follow that example. I made up my mind then that never would I mention money needs. I was not known to anybody except a few people in the North of Ireland, mostly just those at the Donegal Road assembly, and it was just a small assembly of working-class people.

After eleven months in Portugal, I had been able to gather the camping equipment I needed—a cot and a little tent. I also bought a case of sardines that were very cheap and thought that at least with sardines and African "mush," I would not die of starvation. With £24 pounds that Donegal Road had sent me, I bought a third class ticket for Angola.

Q: Now it is seventy years later. Do you still have the two half sovereigns?
A: Yes, I still have them. They are over one hundred years old now.

Q: Don't you think Tommy Robinson would be pleased to know that God has so cared for you that you have not needed to use them?
A: Yes, in all that time, I have never been in debt for one penny and I have never asked or even hinted about money to anyone. During World War II, there was eleven months when the Portuguese would not handle our mail. During all that time we never missed a meal. As I said, in seventy years, we have never been in debt for one penny to anybody.

The story of the sovereigns was not known until at our fiftieth wedding anniversary. Mr. Fred MacKenzie had heard of it and asked me to tell the story. I was able to put my hand in my pocket and produce them for all to see. That night Dr. Bier was there, too, and he presented me with a tin of sardines! It is good to be able to look back and remember the faithfulness of God.

TWENTY-TWO

Captured by the North Vietnamese

Sam Mattix was commended from the USA to Laos in 1971. He took a year's course at the Missionary School of Medicine in London before moving to Kengkok. Along with Lloyd Oppel (commended from Canada in 1972) he was captured by the Viet Cong and held for five months.

In July of 1972 I went to Laos to join missionary friends working there. I started language study and began to learn something about life in Laos. Meanwhile, the war in Viet Nam was still going on just a few miles to the east of us. We often heard distant bombing and gunfire.

October 28, 1972 was the day a proposed cease-fire was to go into effect at 11 AM in Southeast Asia. Henry Kissinger had said on the news the previous day: "Peace is at hand." During the night and early morning hours of October 27-28, Communist forces moved rapidly to take over as much territory as they could before the cease-fire

205

took effect. When my friend Lloyd Oppel and I got up at 5:30 AM on the 28th, we had no idea that Communists troops had advanced into our area during the night. We rose, washed up, and started making breakfast as usual. While I was in front of the stove, a young neighbor man dashed up to our house and told Lloyd that Communists were coming across the rice paddies into the village. Lloyd yelled the word to me to clear out. We deserted the kitchen, grabbed up our travel documents, pulled on our shoes, then took off in Lloyd's Mazda pickup for the town Kengkok, a mile away, where four friends lived.

As we careened out of our driveway, a rifle blast from somewhere behind us in the direction of the advancing troops hurried us on our way. We planned to warn our friends in Kengkok, who were missionaries like ourselves, and to make it to a place where we could be evacuated by helicopter.

Lloyd tromped on the accelerator all the way to Kengkok. We did 60 or 70 mph along the straight gravel stretch. Two groups of soldiers in battle dress let us pass them by. We didn't realize at the time that they were North Vietnamese! At the entrance to Kengkok a large group of soldiers stood guard. As we roared into the intersection, they trained their guns on us. I heard them shouting "Halt! Halt!" but Lloyd kept right on going. Ducking instinctively, I said, "Lloyd, stop!"

CAPTURED BY THE NORTH VIETNAMESE

"Blam! Blam!" Rifle blasts fired just overhead forced Lloyd to comply. Immediately he hit the brakes. We skidded to a stop. Soldiers trotted warily to the sides of the truck, keeping their automatic weapons trained on us. They ordered us to get out of the truck, with our hands up. Guns were put at our backs, we were frisked for weapons and our hands and elbows tied. Next we were tied to the posts of a barbed-wire fence. I glanced at my watch: it was 5:55 AM and the sun was just coming up.

I looked around. More soldiers were coming into the town from various directions. Scouting parties were fanning out into the town. Some were bringing back radio equipment, medicine and food. We expected at any time to see our co-workers being brought up as prisoners too, but they never came. I prayed for their safety and ours, but felt confident that we would be released shortly after the cease-fire took effect later that morning.

Lloyd and I decided to pass time singing about Jesus, partly to let our captors know that we were not afraid and also to reinforce the fact that we were not American agents. We had already told them that we were missionaries who teach about Jesus—that Lloyd was a carpenter and I was a medic—that we were not soldiers—that Lloyd was not even an American but was a Canadian. All this information seemed to have fallen on deaf ears; they continued to guard us warily and keep us tightly bound.

GOD IS FAITHFUL

Around 6:30 AM, saffron-robed Buddhist monks passed with their begging bowls, collecting food on their usual morning rounds. Lloyd and I sang a children's song for them in Lao, telling of the joy we have as Christians.

My guards moved me to a new location inside the fence in the shade, where I could not be spotted from the air. They tied me with rope and thin wire to a clothesline pole. Things had been going quite well up to this point, so I was not too worried.

A GRAVE SITUATION

My feelings changed radically at about 7:30 AM when a soldier came along with a shovel. He broke the turf right between Lloyd and me and began to dig. Soon the shape of the hole became apparent: it was rectangular, about 5 feet long by 2 feet wide with nice straight sides. And the soldier kept digging deeper and deeper. I thought of a recent report from further south in Laos: after Communists overran one town, they took two school teachers, slit their foreheads, gouged out their eyes and then buried them alive. As the shovel dug deeper, my heart was pounding, my mouth dry, my stomach in a knot, my legs feeling weak as if before a race.

The prospect of being shot or buried alive numbed me. Wouldn't they wait for the treaty? Would they kill two civilians without even checking the facts? I visualized being tossed into the hole...the dirt coming down... thudding on my body, cutting off the light...the air. But what afterwards? Death seemed like a door opening into absolute darkness. I thought, "I'm going to heaven" but the words seemed empty and trite as I watched the dirt piling up beside the hole.

"How do I know for sure?" I asked myself. It had been so easy to say that I believed it all when life was safe and death far away. Now the black door of death was opening before me; eternity or the absolute end of existence lay one step away just over the threshold. Again I asked myself, "How do you know that what you believe is right? A lot of wise people, a lot of good people, believe differently from you. What if they are right and you are wrong? What if everyone's wrong?"

In the darkness of my soul at that moment all I could do was stand by faith on this foundation: There is a God who made this world. I know it didn't just happen. It couldn't have. Jesus Christ is a fact of history. He was not just a man; He was much more. He said He was God's Son. He died and He rose again; the witness of history is solid. Experiences of the past year added to my confidence in God. Repeatedly God had given specific answers to my prayers and I had seen convincing evidence of His supernatural care in my life. Also, I knew from study that the Bible is a miraculous book and shows

GOD IS FAITHFUL

the fingerprint of God throughout. (You have to get into the Bible to know it. Most critics never read it!)

I did a lot more serious thinking and praying while that hole was being dug. I pled with the Lord to spare my life so I could keep on living for Him. Lloyd and I talked a little and after a while sang again. After what seemed like ages, the soldier who was digging the hole started to cover it over with brush; then we could see that the hole was not a grave. It was a gun-nest. What a relief!

A lot more happened that day. Three Christian men risked their lives to come and argue with our captors for our release. They were so persistent that they nearly got shot. Lloyd's truck got wrecked by a bunch of soldiers who didn't know how to drive. We were fed some boiled rice and salt and were given dirty water to drink in the afternoon. My glasses were taken away by a tough-talking young soldier. An officer forced us to abandon our shoes. In the afternoon the soldiers weren't so tense; perhaps they felt that the situation was under control. We tried to show friendliness and courage in the presence of all our captors.

Gradually the guards became less wary. One group of soldiers gathered around us and tried to talk to us. One man asked us if we would like to go to Hanoi. We answered "Sure! We'd love to go to Hanoi." It sounded like an adventure, and a better option than execution!

CAPTURED BY THE NORTH VIETNAMESE

At dusk, the North Vietnamese commandeered a local Chinese merchant's truck and loaded us, along with some of the loot from the town, into the back of the truck. That was the start of forty days on the Ho Chi Minh Trail. We traveled on foot for twenty-five days, into the foothills and on up into the mountains. We were under guard at all times and were tied up day and night for the first twenty days. Sometimes we rode trucks at night. We stayed in Lao villages at first, then in army camps along the trail in the jungle, and later in Vietnamese villages.

On the trail we were in constant danger from soldiers and civilians who wanted to do us in because of their hate towards Americans. Lloyd nearly died of malaria during the time on the trail. Finally we arrived at prison in Hanoi; the infamous "Hanoi Hilton." Lloyd got even sicker in prison with beriberi in addition to his malaria. I had bouts with typhus and malaria too.

After we'd been in Hanoi more than a month, we were taken to a small prison outside Hanoi, where we spent three weeks in solitary confinement for interrogation. After the treaty was signed on January 28, 1973, we were moved back to the "Hanoi Hilton" on February 6th and put in with other prisoners.

On March 28, five months to the day after our capture, we were released from prison and flown to Clark AFB in the Philippines and from there we were able to go home in a few days for a wonderful reunion with family and friends.

May I ask you an important question: if you stood beside your grave right now, what confidence would you have? Do you know where you are going when you die? I know it's not very pleasant to think about death, but it's even worse not to. The Bible says: *"It is appointed unto men once to die, but after this the judgment"* (Heb. 9:27). You may still live a long time or you may die today, but you cannot escape the fact that one day you will die.

God says that after you die you will stand before Him and give an account of yourself to Him. As your friend, I want you to know where you stand with God before you die. You're not ready to live until you're ready to die. Please don't take a chance with your life; mean business with God about solving the big question in life. You might only have today to make up your mind. Find out for yourself who Jesus is and what He said; find out by reading the Bible. Matthew, Mark, Luke, or John would be good books in the Bible to read first.

For your own sake find out the truth now for yourself about God, about Jesus Christ, about heaven and hell and about life after death. Jesus promises: *""Ye shall know the truth, and the truth shall make you free...If the Son therefore shall make you free, ye shall be free indeed"* (Jn. 8:32, 36).

TWENTY-THREE

Great is Thy Faithfulness

Gordon and Florence Wakefield were commended in 1964 to the Lord and His work in Peru by the assembly in Hutchinson, Kansas. For 38 years they have sought to serve the Lord and His people in the capital city of Lima (pop. 1,750,000 when they arrived; now over 8 million). On arrival, they served with and learned from two missionary couples. Over the years they have participated with other missionaries and nationals in the ministries of seven assemblies planted in the city, while also being responsible for the Emmaus Bible Correspondence School for 23 years (now in other hands) and the direction of an evening Bible institute for the past 27 years.

Malignant melanoma! A new word had entered our family's vocabulary, a synonym for fear.

It was February 1973 and we had been on the mission field in Lima, Peru for nine years. It had been more than long enough to prove the confidence we had put in the

Lord. After eleven years of praying, asking, listening, waiting, we had heard the Lord's clear call and had been commended by the small assembly in Hutchinson, Kansas, to put all aside and launch out, taking our three children to an unfamiliar land to serve an unknown people in the gospel.

Well we remembered how the elders in our commending assembly expressed their concerns for our financial support. We had appreciated their thoughts as they tried to put into proper perspective the few believers in the assembly, the small monthly missionary offerings, and the cost of maintaining a family of five in the metropolis that was Lima. We had sympathized with the elders, but assured them we were looking to the Lord of the Harvest for our needs and to the assembly for its prayers.

THE CALL

Now, nine years later, on a typical day in Lima, came the telephone call. Melanoma! It was the voice of Richard Burson, an elder in our commending assembly, a full-time worker and also guardian for our oldest, Tom, 18, studying in the local junior college. His message? The spot on Tom's back that had been excised four months earlier had returned, and had been diagnosed as malignant melanoma. Then came the doctor's observation: he had had 15 melanoma patients in 20 years of practice; it was a particularly virulent form of cancer; all but two of his patients had died of the dread disease. It was recommended that Tom be taken to the M. D. Anderson cancer research hospital in Houston, Texas, immediately. The rest of the conversation with Richard was received in a haze and fades from memory.

When I had answered that phone call I had heard the "beep" that always signals an international call, and therefore had called to Florence. She was at my side listening to my responses during the conversation and, of course, could sense the seriousness of the matter without knowing the details. A hurried explanation to her was followed by calling our other children, Paul, 16, and Elizabeth, 15, to the living room where all was explained and where we prayed, committing Tom and ourselves to the Lord for whatever was to follow.

Only then came the realization of the extra income we would need to provide for these added expenses!

THAT EXTRA INCOME

The first year we were in Peru we were grateful to note that our financial support for that year was exactly equal to my salary as a public school teacher the year before we went to Peru. We had thanked God for His faithfulness and for thus demonstrating that He would not do less for us than He had done while we were in secular work. We had, indeed, experienced some months of "no extras" in our family, but always enough. *"My God shall supply all your NEED...."*

In the face of so much need in Peru we had even been able to increase the percentage of our giving which Florence and I had covenanted with the Lord to pass on directly into His work and for some of the needs of the Peruvian believers. And we knew that it is in such a context of sharing with others that the Apostle Paul states that principle/promise in Philippians 4:19.

Yes, the extra income! As we began to settle into the reality of the situation with Tom, our need to be with him, to guide him through whatever experiences lay ahead, to comfort, to encourage, to share and to learn, we began to make plans. Foremost in our minds was the considerable cost of air fares for four people.

But, there was that extra income! For each of the three months prior to the phone call from Tom's guardian we had been surprised by a noticeable increase in support. The first month Florence and I had merely commented on it, with thanksgiving. The second month of such increase in support we had wondered aloud what the Lord had in mind, and had even mentioned one or two possible "projects" we had talked of related to our ministries in Peru. But the third month of considerable increase of funds we really knew that the Lord had a definite purpose in mind and it was for us to wait and see what it might be.

Now we knew. *"It shall come to pass that before they call, I will answer"* (Isa. 65:24). Now we understood. We gave thanks again to our faithful God, purchased the airline tickets and packed our suitcases.

Of course, the experience of God's provision in unusual circumstances did not end there, though the provision for that amount was sufficient in itself to give testimony to His glory, testimony which we have happily given many times over the years.

At that time we did not have medical insurance. We had been directed to the cancer research center in Texas, a facility with over 700 outpatients per day, all with one or another form of cancer.

We arrived in Houston about the same time Tom's grandparents arrived with him from Kansas. In a special time of prayer with our gracious hosts, Stan and Marilyn Boyer, and the elders from their assembly, we committed Tom to the Lord for His all-wise and all-loving care, and began what was to be 18 months of hospital visits, doctors' consultations, experimental treatments, much more prayer, abundant tears and, ALWAYS, God's faithfulness.

DAY BY DAY

Almost our first "hurdle" was not with the disease itself but with the business office of the hospital. As it had been almost ten years since we had any dealings with hospitals in the U.S., we were totally innocent of what it meant for a patient to approach a hospital for treatment without medical insurance.

When our "financial situation" became clear to the business office (meaning no insurance, missionaries by profession, no mission board, no guaranteed salary, residents of a foreign country), there was considerable consultation by the hospital authorities with the final decision that Tom would be accepted as a patient only if daily expenses could be settled on a daily basis. Could we accept such a condition? Yes, we could, but it was not just because we had no alternative. It was because we had an ever faithful God who had prepared us "before [we] called..." for just this moment and circumstance.

There followed 18 months of doctors' fees, hospital fees, in-patient, out-patient, experimental treatments, travel expenses, etc. Expenses were indeed paid daily. Thousands of dollars passed through our hands. The money was always there. There were tears—tears for Tom and tears of thankfulness for God's presence and His provision. In addition, there was the loving and sacrificial response of many believers in the Braeburn assembly and the Spanish speaking assembly in Houston with supportive visits, homes opened for our time spent in Houston and vehicles always at our disposal.

But there was another supply. As commitment and confidence increased, peace increased. As we saw we lacked nothing, our thankfulness grew. We learned to share the truth of those lines of Florence's favorite missionary poet, Amy Carmichael, "In acceptance lieth peace...." And this, after all, was the most important provision of our faithful God.

Eighteen months passed. No treatment produced positive results. A temporary delay of the advance of the dread disease came now and then, but it was a downhill progression all the way. Tom's body did not respond, and eventually his super-alert and super-keen mind began to falter along with his body. An avid reader, he found he could not concentrate on the one activity he loved most. Well we remember the last lucid conversation he had with us when, with child-like simplicity he asked, "Do you think God still wants me in this condition?" Tom was saved and baptized and taken into fellowship at an early age and we could assure him that God not only would have him, but was eager to have him, and that it was *"far better"* to be with Christ.

Once the disease had metastasized to the brain, the end was near. That is, the end of the earthly part. On July 13, 1974, at the age of 19, Tom entered into full life. His ordeal was over. We had learned many lessons, and we had been confirmed in our convictions. *"His compas-*

sions fail not. They are new every morning; GREAT IS THY FAITHFULNESS" (Lam. 3:23).

TWENTY-FOUR

God Will Take Care of You

George and Emma Wiseman were commended from the States to the Lord's work in Angola in 1936. During the period of terrorist activity, they spent five years in Harare, Zimbabwe where they undertook the printing and distribution of tracts in various languages, the average annual output being 2,500,000. They returned to Biula (Angola) and the Chokwe work in 1969. Emma died the following year.

In the early thirties, Mr. Malcolm McJanet, who had been a missionary in Angola for some years, gave a report in Grace Gospel Chapel, Jersey City, of the Lord's work among the Chokwe people in the northeast of Angola. He described a large unevangelized area called Camaxilo, and asked his hearers to pray the Lord to send workers to take the Gospel there.

About the same time, another esteemed missionary in Angola, Mr. T. E. Wilson, spoke in the Dwight Street

Gospel Chapel, New Jersey. He too emphasized the great need in such areas where the gospel was not known.

It was through these reports that, as time passed, I was increasingly exercised and interested in the unevangelized area of Camaxilo. These events, we believe, were of God, and this is the story of God's faithfulness and providence in answering the prayers of His people, and supplying all that was necessary for the spread of the gospel to that area.

My wife and I left New York in November 1935, bound for Angola. We travelled by sea to Britain, and from there to Lobito, 250 miles south of the capital Luanda; a journey of 29 days in total. From there we travelled by train to the town of Luena in the interior, and on by truck to the Mission Station at Buila, in the heart of Chokwe country. Shortly after arriving in Chokweland, we met a young missionary, Mr. R. C. Allison from Scotland. He too had a similar exercise about the Carnaxilo area to the north, having heard from Mr. Wilson of that unevangelized part.

It was to be ten years, however, before we had the joy and privilege of going there. Those were years of gaining experience with senior missionaries, learning the Chokwe language, and proving God's faithfulness in many ways. They were also difficult years, for World War II was in progress, and communication with the outside world was poor. But during those days I was reminded of lines from a hymn, heard in my unconverted youth in Ireland, when it was sung by a young woman at an open air meeting:

> *Be not dismayed whate'er betide,*
> *God will take care of you.*

Seventy years have passed since then, and His care has never failed.

Travel to the Camaxilo area was impossible without a suitable vehicle, which we did not have. On our first furlough I was invited to give a missionary report at Yonkers assembly in New York. At that meeting I met a brother in the Lord who had a great interest in missionary work. Within a few days a gift arrived, earmarked for a vehicle for our work. A short time later we received from the same brother a further gift, the total being sufficient to purchase a three-quarter ton Chevy pickup. Such was God's provision.

At that time, with the war not long over, it was difficult to obtain such vehicles, but "God has servants everywhere." One of them was in General Motors' office in New York City, and was used by God to ensure that when we returned to Angola, we collected our new truck.

In March of 1948, Crawford Allison, Donald McLeod, two African brothers and I started on the first journey to Camaxilo—about 500 miles north of the mission station at Buila. God had brought about all the circumstances whereby the prayers of His servants would be answered. What a journey and what a privilege to take the light of the gospel to a people who sat in darkness.

Visits to the area continued twice yearly, and each time we were able to reach new villages. God blessed His Word, and in 1951 some were baptized and the first assembly planted at Camaxilo.

God's timing is always perfect, and the story of the planting of the first assembly in Camaxilo illustrates this. A few natives of Camaxilo had gone from an early age with their parents to work in the cocoa plantations on St. Thomas Island in the Gulf of Guinea off the west coast of Africa. While there they heard the gospel from a Portuguese missionary, and were saved. They returned to the mainland, grown men, in 1947. It was a happy day for them and us when, around 1949, we met at Camaxilo, never having heard of each other before. We had the pleasure of baptizing them, and they formed the nucleus of that first assembly.

That was just the beginning of the work of the Holy Spirit at Camaxilo. Africans, saved by the grace of God, took the gospel in later years (1959 and after) to thousands of their own people, so that today there are over 200 assemblies in that area, and the neighboring areas of Cafunfo and Xinji. Truly it can be said of them, *"from you sounded out the Word of the Lord."* A number of our fellow-workers visited Camaxilo at times, and gave much valuable help.

Thus did God, in His own time, and in His own way, fulfill His Word: *"...according to this time it shall be said of Jacob and of Israel, What hath God wrought!"* (Num. 23:23).

TWENTY-FIVE

When the Circus Came to Town

John W. Bramhall was born in Sheffield, England in 1899. With his parents, he migrated to New York in 1911. He was saved in 1914 through the ministry of Harold Harper, probably his first convert. Called to the pioneer work of the Lord in 1934, Mr. Bramhall labored in South Carolina for a decade before the Lord broadened his ministry to include Canada, the US and the West Indies. All this while, he maintained daily radio programs for Bible exposition in North and South Carolina.

Circus day in Dixie 1934! The local town folks and countryside were excited! There was a circus parade on Saturday morning with hundreds of spectators along the route. What a great opportunity to give out gospel tracts. So fortified with the good seed, I made my way all along the route, oblivious to the animals and clowns and circus performers. Hundreds of tracts were distributed. Then I returned to pass out my little good news messengers to the crowds streaming into the afternoon and evening performances. I arrived late back home, exhausted and conscious of a backache, but with a prayer on my lips for God's blessing of the day's labor for Him.

The county fair followed the circus for a week, with another opportunity to spend each day distributing tracts, offering Bibles for twenty-five cents and New Testaments for five cents, in the heart of the Great Depression.

The southern states were still segregated at that time. Another week was extended at the county fair, granted to the black citizens to enjoy the exhibits, together with an adjoining carnival. Once more the daily sowing of the "good seed" went on, and thousands of tracts were given out on these occasions, fulfilling the scripture, *"In the morning sow thy seed, and in the evening withhold not thy hand: for thou knowest not which shall prosper"* (Eccl. 11:6). Eternity will reveal it all, but God graciously gives encouragement now!

An aged man, followed by five children who were asking him for money, drew near to the exhibition building where I was distributing tracts. He asked if I could give him change for a quarter; I readily granted his request. Giving the youngsters a dime to run off and spend, he said, "I want to talk to this gentleman." Said he, "Brother! You are the man who was giving out those tickets at the big show the other night. You gave me one and I read it. I said, 'That's just what my people need,' and I looked for you all over but never found you. But I picked up all that I could find on the ground," for many had thrown them away in rejection.

"Lord, I wish he would follow me everywhere," I thought.

"Brother," he continued, "one night my aunt sent for me. She ran a boarding house, and had a man who was dying. 'Could you help him?' she asked. I went over and that man was dying and he was afraid to die!

"Brother," he said, "I had one of those tickets left in my vest pocket—so I read it to him and said, 'Believe it and you will die happy.' I told him, 'Some man at the big show gave some to me. I don't know who he was and suppose he went on with the show!' After reading the tract I gave it to him and said, 'If you read this and believe it, you'll die happy!'"

Then with a broad grin on his face, the old man looked up to me and said, "Brother, that man DIED HAPPY!"

As the old man turned to go, I silently prayed in thanksgiving, "Lord, thank You for the backache."

Sow, sow, sow; you may not see it grow,
Scatter seeds of precious truth, everywhere you go.
Sow, sow, sow; and God will fruit bestow;
And it will keep your heart aglow—
So—Sow! Sow! Sow!

TWENTY-SIX

Can God Supply an Engine in the Wilderness?

David Long moved from Belfast in 1934 to help T. E. Wilson in Angola. The next year Eleanor Archibald came from Canada and the two were married. In 1939, they moved to Kapango and later to Luma where they labored for many years. David was instrumental in building up the Bible school which attracted young men from the entire Chokwe area. He completed a translation of the Chokwe Bible. The Long's were forced to evacuate at the end of 1967.

In sixty years of full-time work for a faithful God it is hard to select an example of His providential care from a lifetime of miracles. There has, however, been one case which has always stood out in my own mind.

My wife Eleanor and I were expecting our first child in early February of 1938. We would have to get to Boma to have Dr. Bier's help, and we would also have to aim at arriving well ahead of time. This was because December and January are the worst months of the rainy season when the roads would be a wallow of mud; rivers would be swollen; and some of the stick bridges would almost certainly be washed out. We were dependent on the 1931 model "A" Ford pickup which the Wilsons had very kindly given us as our transportation link with the outside world when they left us for a much needed furlough almost a year earlier. We had been completely alone during this time in one of the most primitive and isolated spots in all of Africa.

There was no direct road from our home at Chitutu to Boma: virgin forest, bush, and swampy plains only. There were two ways we could go, but either way we had to travel three sides of a square to get there. One of these would be 540 miles, the other 650; all over dirt tracks and with little hope of help in case of breakdown or accident. Our trust simply had to be in the Lord since there was nothing and no one else.

CAR TROUBLE

About six weeks before our planned trip I had to go to the railhead at Malange for some much needed supplies. On the way back, overloaded as usual, the engine blew a cylinder-head gasket. Since I failed to diagnose the prob-

AN ENGINE IN THE WILDERNESS?

lem I set about stripping down the whole unit. In putting it back together the oil pump was not properly seated and, when I started up the engine, the pump fell out of place and the crankshaft drove it out through the side of the engine block, leaving a gaping hole.

My feelings can be imagined when it is understood that so far as we knew, this was the only car of its kind at that early date in the whole of Angola. Indeed it was the only vehicle of any kind in our part of the country apart from that of the District Officer at the Post five miles away, and that was a Chevrolet. Hope of even finding an engine block would be about as reasonable as looking for a camel at the North Pole. And even if we found such a block and had the money to buy it (which we did not), no motor mechanic to put it all together had ever been seen or heard of in our part of Africa.

We had more than our share of troubles of every sort in our almost five years in Africa, but never anything so shattering as this. It was a dead end, and the only thing we could think of was the dreaded business of having Eleanor carried in a hammock by relays of men on what would be at least a fourteen day trek to Boma overland—with those swollen rivers, washed out bridges, flooded plains, and sleeping in a tent. I can assure you we sent up some real distress calls to the Man in Glory even though there seemed no way out.

GOD IS FAITHFUL

A STRING OF MIRACLES

The Administrative Officer at the Post had heard of our predicament and—miracle number one—it happened that he had brought overland from Bié (pronounced *bee'aye*), out nearer the coast, a couple of motor mechanics to overhaul his pick-up. He kindly brought them down to our place to have a look at my problem. When they saw the hole in the side of the engine they just shook their heads and said the only answer was a whole new engine block.

Then—miracle number two—one of them remembered that some time before they had bought the remains of a similar Ford which had been wrecked at a railway crossing and which they had towed away on the off chance that they might some day be able to use some of the parts. The engine had not been damaged; it was in good condition; and they would sell it to me for £25 installed (at that time a little over $100).

For me there were two big obstacles here. 1) The engine was in Bié and there was no car available to fetch it even if the dirt roads were passable and, 2) I did not have the £25.

The Portuguese officer immediately said that he would take a bunch of Africans off free government road work and send them on foot to Bié to carry the engine back lashed to poles! While I turned this seemingly impossible job over in my mind, I was forced, with keen embarrass-

AN ENGINE IN THE WILDERNESS?

ment to confess that even if that could be done I did not have the £25 anyway. It was one of the most painful moments in my whole life. Here was the engine I needed so badly; probably the only other Ford engine of that type in the whole of Angola; and I had to confess to strangers and unconverted men that I did not have the necessary, though trifling, money for it.

With typical Portuguese kindness and generosity the officer immediately offered to lend me the money which I could pay back any time it suited me, but of course I could not do this. I explained how we did not receive a regular wage but were supported by Christians and living by faith in God, and that we had no idea if or when such a sum might come our way. I knew, and he knew, that mail only came at best every two weeks and frequently with gaps of more than two months between, so I had to decline his offer. I felt I had no choice, yet it was a humiliation to have to confess it to them all. After some more coaxing that we should accept and let him send the men immediately (since it would take them at least a week to walk out to Bié and possibly two weeks more to prepare the load and bring it back), I had to let them go back to the Post while Eleanor and I sat down and wept.

Two days later the officer came down all excited to tell me that an unexpected mail runner had come in from his superior at the Administration and with the official papers there was a letter for us which had apparently been left over from a previous mail. Very pleased, he said, "Open it up; there'll be money in it." I had little hope and was also afraid that if I opened it and there was no money it would be too much to bear in front of him. He, however, insisted and in the letter was the equivalent of £30. He said he would exchange the dollars into Portuguese Escudos and make all the arrangements.

Off he went and called up three local chiefs and told them to gather up between them eighteen men who would take a letter to Bié. Those there would wrap the engine block in a tarpaulin, sling it onto a pole with three cross bars which they would have cut out of the forest. They would then head back to him at the Post full speed, six men carrying at a time, six resting (while they walked of course), and six going ahead with axes to cut out shrubs or trees to widen the native path sufficiently to allow them through. He gave them a lengthy, and to us, embarrassing lecture on all we missionaries had done for them and now they must do their best to help us out. He also said that if they got back quickly they would be given an extra tip, and if they did not, he would give them an extra month of roadwork! Those were still the "bad old days" but there was nothing we could do about this part of the business.

The Christians at the mission helped us push our pick-

AN ENGINE IN THE WILDERNESS?

up the five miles or so to the Post, mostly uphill; the mechanics pulled the old engine out and stripped all the parts off the block so that when the other one arrived they could reassemble everything.

The exhausted men arrived three weeks later with the engine and the mechanics worked night and day to put it all together, test drive it, and hand it over to us.

We packed our things and left for Boma but the roads were so bad and we had to dig the car out so often that in four days we could only make it to Bié near the East-West railway line. Here we left the pick-up at Monte Esperanca with our missionary colleagues there and took the train to Luso where Dr. Bier picked us up; and so to Boma.

As it turned out our calculations were wrong (it was our first child and there were no prenatal classes and examinations) so we had to wait a week or two while the good doctor drove my wife over every bumpy road and bridge in the vicinity with extra doses of quinine to try to speed things on a bit. Finally, on the last day of February, Patrick was born, though I have wondered if he realizes what he put us through.

MORE ENGINE TROUBLE

Five years later, in the United States and two days before I must be back across the border into Canada, another engine blew up with a broken crankshaft which also knocked the side out of that engine halfway between Detroit and Grand Rapids. Those were the war years when everything was strictly limited on a military priority basis. Yet in just as miraculous a way as before, God supplied a new engine, had it installed again, and I got back over the border on the last day of my thirty-day visitor's permit. So it really is what Dickens might have called "A tale of two engines," though the second one just as strange and full of the mystery of God's providential care and power as the first, will not fit in this paper.

In present days it would seem that in many minds commendation means a commitment to support with a stated number of dollars per month. My little story shows that all the gold in Fort Knox (if indeed it is still there) would not have solved my problem. The Lord had to supply an engine in the wilderness. We limit God when we imagine we can solve everything with dollars. The simple fact is—we cannot. In such emergencies, only God will do.

TWENTY-SEVEN

God Always has Someone

Madge Beckon sailed for China in April of 1947 with her late husband, Gifford, and infant daughter, Ruth. While they were serving in Kweiyang, Kweichow, their daughter, Esther, was born. In 1949, because of Communist activity in China, they were evacuated to Hong Kong and later spent six months in Taiwan. In 1951, their third daughter, Eunice, was born shortly after they moved to Takasaki, Gunma Ken. This was their home as long as they were in Japan (38 years for Madge). Gifford and Madge worked as a team until the Lord took him home in 1974. Madge continued in Japan until 1987.

Have you ever noticed the number of times it is recorded in Scripture that God prepared various things or people for special service to Himself ahead of when it would be really needed? Some of these He created for the particular purpose such as a fish, a gourd, a worm and an east wind. (These are examples taken from the book of Jonah alone and there are others.) But it is not fish and worms that I am thinking about, but special people that God has used to fill the personal needs of the saints. It is astounding when I think back over the years how often God has prepared a person to be there just when I have needed them the most. God always has someone! This has been especially true since I became a widow, but I am getting ahead of myself and will tell some of our experiences from when we first arrived in China in 1947.

IN JOURNEYINGS OFT

Gifford was held up in Shanghai getting our baggage through customs so we thought it would be wise for me to start ahead of him by ship up the Yangtze River and he was to follow by plane. I was traveling with a veteran missionary family to the port closest to their mission station where I would wait for Gifford to join me.

The first week of traveling all went on schedule as planned, then our three-month-old baby, Ruth, got dysentery from the water and was one sick little girl. By the time we arrived at the port, her drastic weight loss made her look like a shriveled-up old lady and I was very alarmed by seeing blood in her stools. We made it to the mission compound and into the hands of a missionary nurse, but it was evident we urgently needed to get her to a doctor. All the missionaries showed much concern and a lot of prayer went up for her.

Arrangements were immediately made for air tickets for Ruthie and I to fly to Chungking for medical help; Gifford was able to get a ticket from Shanghai on the same plane. A co-worker from our station was to meet us in Chungking and to act as interpreter as I spoke no Chinese and Gifford had forgotten his during high school, college, and Air Force days. Reservations were made to stay at the C.I.M. mission home and everything possible had been thought of and worked out in detail—all but the weather, that is.

I met Gifford's plane at Nangking and we boarded on schedule, feeling confident and relaxed since we were a family again and would soon have Ruth in the hands of a good doctor. The plane was a troop-transport with passengers lined against the sides and baggage tied down to the floor in the center. We sure didn't have any of the comforts of modern plane travel, but this was no problem as we were grateful to be on our way. It didn't even bother me that I never heard a single word of English the whole trip, apart from our own conversation, for I felt assured that we would be met in Chungking.

Our first alarm came when we arrived at the airport and there was no foreigner to meet us as we had expected. Our second concern was that we had not touched down in the city of Chungking but rather on an island with a wide river separating us from our destination. There had been no message of explanation from anyone so by this time I was really getting uneasy. After a long wait and not understanding what was going on, we noticed a ferry approaching from the other side of the river. When everyone boarded the ferry and someone motioned us to do the same, we followed suit, hoping we would still see an American face at the other end.

Just before the ferry reached the dock, a well-dressed Chinese gentleman approached us and asked in perfect English, "What is your baby's name?" He had actually heard our conversation on the plane and later at the airport, and had been aware of our consternation all along. But he hadn't been sure whether to offer help or not. He then assured us that if there was no one in Chungking to help us, he would hire a rickshaw which would take us to the mission home; he knew where it was. From our conversation he surmised that we lacked the language to hire a rickshaw and therefore could not give the rickshaw man directions or barter for the fare.

He turned out to be a very kind, friendly person and he was true to his word. When we reached the shore he wrote out instruction in Chinese, taking money from our hand to pay the man at the other end and letting the man know he was not to overcharge us. Here was a man returning from the U.S. to inland China but I firmly believe he was sent by God to be on the right plane to save the life of a very sick baby and to help two very frantic parents. What perfect timing when we needed it most! I wanted so badly to hug as we parted, but I didn't dare.

Soon after we arrived, a message came from our missionary friend who had promised to meet us. He explained that he had been held up by a flood and couldn't cross the river until the water level came down. He had no idea how long he would have to wait before he could meet us. But this turned out to be of the Lord. The extra time was needed to treat Ruthie

She was cared for by a missionary doctor who was an expert in these types of diseases and was staying in Chungking at the time. This was not chance, either, but a direct provision of the Lord. By the time the missionary arrived to escort us to our mission station, Ruthie was well on the way to recovery. She had responded very well in answer to the many prayers.

We had two-and-a-half very happy years working in fellowship with the missionary family in Kweiyang, Kweichow. Those years are good memories.

Then one day we received a letter from the American Embassy, ordering us to leave China immediately because our city was completely surrounded by the Communist army. We were again on the move, flying to Hong

Kong this time. We had planned to go directly to Japan but had found in transit that we were not allowed to enter Japan with a young baby under a year old since the living conditions were still so poor after the war. We had to wait until our second daughter, Esther was a year old.

Hong Kong was flooded with immigrants from all over China so we decided it would be better to wait in Taiwan. We had no trouble renting a house in Taipei. Then we were faced with a new problem. After the expensive traveling out of China into Taiwan, paying a huge deposit on the house, and setting up house keeping, our resources were greatly depleted. Our mail was not coming through because no one in the States had been able to keep up with our plans which had changed so suddenly. We soon found ourselves in an extremely distressing and embarrassing situation.

POWER FROM ON HIGH

One day our electric bill had been delivered and we were not able to pay it. Gifford had called for an extension of grace but was refused and told that our electricity would be shut off the next day at noon. After the phone call and a good time of prayer, Gifford and I decided to go for a walk, leaving the two children with a single missionary. Not three blocks from home we met a believer from the local church who was also trying to find relief from the intense summer heat in the cool of the evening. We had a very nice time of fellowship as he joined us.

When we parted, he pulled something from his pocket, saying that he had received a letter from a friend in America that day. His friend had enclosed a twenty dollar bill which he said was illegal for him to cash so he slipped it into Gifford's hand, asking him to please cash it and use it. This time I wanted to burst into tears instead of hugging him but again I restrained myself. We returned home with much praise and thanksgiving. The twenty dollars more then covered the electric bill and gave us a little extra besides.

THE BIG FAT LETTER

One more crisis which comes to mind happened a few years after Gifford passed away. I don't feel free to share any of the details with you but I was going through a difficult time spiritually and emotionally. That day we were at an all-day affair of the local church when, about noon, I succumbed completely to a spirit I knew was certainly not from the Lord. I was so overcome with self-pity and discouragement that I had to leave the service to return home in defeat.

I had no more than walked in the door when the mailman arrived, leaving a big, fat letter from my sister. I didn't have much heart to read it, but I opened it anyway.

GOD IS FAITHFUL

I found the letter to be full of love and warm, encouraging news from home about the whole family. She closed by reconfirming her love and stressed the fact that everybody at home was praying for me. Being deeply touched, in the privacy of my own study, I freely released the fountain of tears that had been building up all morning. After a time of prayer and confession, I felt much better.

I confessed to the Lord that I had been consumed with self-pity and had forgotten His great love for me which He very clearly expressed through my sister. I felt so light-hearted that I returned to my Christian friends and actually enjoyed the rest of the day.

Whether it's a language barrier, dire financial needs or emotional and spiritual problems, I can say with assurance that God has always had someone to help when I have needed it. God has proven Himself *"a very present help in trouble"* (Ps. 41:1). He often does this through people. I pray that I will always be prepared and available to help in His plan by being the human arm or a mouth He wants to use in ministering to someone else.

TWENTY-EIGHT

He Will Do It!

Joyce E. Finch, trained as a nurse, was commended from the US in 1966 to serve the Lord in medical work at Chavuma, Zambia. She is also involved in assembly activities and outreach.

It was a cool, crisp day, the day after Thanksgiving in November of 1966. The ship slowly left the dock in Brooklyn, New York. What was ahead of me? I knew the Lord promised never to leave me nor forsake me (Heb. 13:5). I also knew the Scripture said that *"He who calls you is faithful, who also will do it"* (1 Thess. 5:24) and that He clothed and fed the birds of the air. My heavenly Father knew that I had, and would have in the future, needs that He knew better than I myself (Mt. 6:25-34). However, until this time I had been an employed person, getting a paycheck which took care of my needs. I was in happy assembly fellowship, owned a car, paid my rent each month and had no bills hanging over my head. In a situation like this one begins to feel quite independent and capable.

I really had no idea how the Lord would look after me. There were friends and family who reinforced the fact that I was not going alone. They promised to pray for me. One even reminded me that we knew the One who owned the cattle on a thousand hills (Ps. 50:2), that I only needed to ask and that He would provide.

Well, the commendation was given, my bags were packed, farewells were said. Two months and some days after departing from New York, I did arrive at Chavuma with all my earthly goods as well as some hospital supplies packed into seven drums.

THE FIRST BIG LESSON

Once at Chavuma I did not have to wait long for the first big lesson on how God would care for me. There have been so many more examples that a book could be filled, but this very first one has never lost its force. I know it was used by God to show me right from the start that He really was in control and very interested in looking after me.

I could not even say that it was a result of much direct prayer on my part concerning the need. God wanted me to know from the start that His faithfulness was not due

HE WILL DO IT!

to anything that I had done. He, for His great name's sake, would care for me.

One of the projects in progress when I arrived at Chavuma was building the foundation and erecting a sixteen thousand gallon water storage tank. The tank, in big sections, had been given by a businessman in South Africa. As I remember it, the only responsibility Chavuma had was to take care of the transportation, the cost of the foundation, and then getting it put together.

One day each of the missionaries was presented with an envelope. In each envelope was a "bill" stating our share of this project. I was a bit shocked, to say the least, and wondered how I was going to take care of this. I did not speak about it with anyone.

By today's standards the amount was not large and I had left a small amount in a checking account in the States—but not enough for this. The nearest phone was 500 miles away. Our mail was very erratic due to our remoteness, and at that time the postal clerks in our local post office were being disciplined and transferred quite regularly. There had been no mail for some time.

But the day after this famous bill was placed in my hand, mail was delivered—on a Sunday! I received a check which would cover the amount I was needing, with a bit left over. The check had left the States several weeks before and arrived just when it was needed. I gave thanks to the Lord and have never forgotten this incident.

Things have changed somewhat over the years. Phones and faxes are now within fifty-two miles of Chavuma. There are only three hundred miles of gravel and dirt in the total five hundred miles of road leading out to the towns. The challenges are still here.

PROVISIONS LARGE AND SMALL

During my time here in Zambia I have seen God provide little things like gloves and thermometers for the hospital, and very large items such as vehicles and a house—without my ever having to ask anyone for anything. The house is a long story, but the Lord allowed us to purchase the building materials bit by bit. I never thought that I would own or consider building a house, and could not even think of the total cost before it was started. I was encouraged by co-workers to look to the Lord. They would supervise the Zambian builders to get it all put together.

First the door and window frames were brought in from town. On another trip with the big truck, a load of cement was acquired. Eventually, the roofing.

While on one of the buying trips for building and hospital supplies, we quite unexpectedly met a missionary with whom we were acquainted but did not see often. These folk lived in the town where we were shopping. We mentioned that we had been around to the auction to look at furniture for a house we were building.

"Oh," said the lady, "we're leaving Zambia. We will be selling all of our furniture. I'll speak to my husband. Come by our house this afternoon. Maybe there are some things you would want."

We were able to buy almost all of their furniture. With no effort on our part, we were able to furnish our new little home with better things than we could have found at the auction. The furniture was the right size, too. The round dining room table was perfect. Our little dining area could not have held another table better. Those missionaries were so pleased to sell everything so quickly and we were thrilled to have our house all outfitted in one go—in the middle of the African bush!

TIRED IN THE MIDDLE OF NOWHERE

For a number of years, our transportation—personal and hospital—has been a one-and-a-half ton pickup truck with a nice high metal canopy fitted at the back. Having frugal genes, I could never travel back to Chavuma with less than a full truck because there are always supplies needed, especially for the hospital.

I was on yet another journey in from the Copperbelt a couple of years ago. We were three missionary ladies. We had left Chingola at about 7:00 in the morning. The first

GOD IS FAITHFUL

200 kilometers on the tarmac road went by quickly. We made a stop at the Provincial Medical headquarters and then were on our way again. Shortly after that stop, the tar ends and the dust began to billow out behind the vehicle. In another hour or so, we began to look for a large tree along the side of the road which might produce a bit of shade under which we could park our truck. There were lots of sparse trees and bush, but there wasn't a lot of shade as the noonday sun beat down on us.

Well, we finally found a spot, enjoyed our picnic lunch, cold drink and coffee, and were on our way again.

About 2:30 in the afternoon, the two others were dozing. I thought the wind must have picked up because the truck seemed to be swaying a bit. Better stop and check the tires. This thought was just in the process when there was a loud bang. The right rear tire had blown out!

Within seconds, it seemed, there was another loud explosion as the left rear tire blew. My hands gripped the steering wheel as we swerved and rocked. I called out to the Lord for help. The driver education course from my high school days came to me, "Turn into the skid." The truck pivoted on the right rear rim. We stopped in the driving lane as though we were returning to town. We could have been upside down in the bush.

Well, here we were, seemingly in the middle of nowhere: three ladies, two badly mangled tires, and a

HE WILL DO IT!

loaded and now very low lying vehicle. But we did have three spare tires!

After some time a Zambian couple came by. He with his axe kindly chopped a few blocks of wood on which to rest the jacks. But two jacks and blocks of wood did not help us much. We would get the truck raised just slightly when the jack would skid on the gravel. The vehicle would settle back to where we had started.

This went on in the heat of the Zambian sun for about an hour. But what was that in the distance? Yes, a vehicle was coming. It slowed and stopped, leaving us all in a cloud of dust. Out jumped four strong, young, Zambian men with a beautiful (to us) two-ton jack. With very little effort the damaged tires were off, spares were put on, and they even removed the shredded tires from the rims so that we could just throw the rims into the back. Not even a bar of soap was accepted as a tip. Before long they were gone off in another cloud of dust. We turned the vehicle around to continue our onward journey with very grateful hearts to God.

HIS PROMISES ARE "YEA" AND "AMEN"

It was only recently that I found the following quote by Charles Spurgeon. "If you have a divine promise, you need not plead it with an 'if'; you may urge it with certainty. The Lord meant to fulfill the promise or He would not have given it. God does not give His words merely to quiet us and to keep us hopeful for awhile with the intention of putting us off at last; but when He speaks, it is because He means to do as He has said" (C. H. Spurgeon in *Morning and Evening*, April 18, evening reading). That sums it all up very succinctly. The Lord is faithful. What He says He will do.

"O taste and see that the Lord is good: blessed is the man that trusteth in Him. O fear the Lord, ye His saints; for there is no want to them that fear Him" (Ps. 34:8-9).

TWENTY-NINE

The Farm and the School

Della Letkeman served with her husband Bill in Colombia and later in Ecuador until returning to Canada where they serve with Everyday Publications. In this chapter, a convert of the work in Colombia tells this story to her.

A father in Medellin, Colombia, desperate to change the course of his son's rebellion, bought Christian literature from foreign missionaries as he left his factory. At home, he found his son, Lucho, listening to the latest Beatles record, and tossed the books at him. "Take these and read them! They might do you some good!"

Lucho picked up a book and read the title, *Can We Know God?* After reading it, he studied a free Emmaus course and began to meet with a young missionary to discuss the Bible. In time, Lucho accepted Christ as his personal Saviour. Later he was baptized and became an active member of an assembly near the university where he was attending.

Ten years later, this babe in Christ had matured spiritually and sensed the Lord's call to work in Bolivia. Upon his arrival, he met and married a petite missionary, Lorna Frood, commended from Scotland. Eventually, Lorna took Lucho to Scotland to meet her family, friends and acquaintances. The Christians provided a Missionary House for them and their two sons in the town of Newarthill, Lanarkshire. Many missionary families had used this home since the 1940s.

Every morning, as Lucho walked to buy a newspaper he passed a Gospel Hall. "It must be an assembly," he told Lorna. "Let's get to know the brethren there."

One summer morning, as he went as usual to the corner store, he noticed that the Gospel Hall had its door slightly ajar. He entered and saw a few seniors praying. Startled, they turned around and gasped when they saw a large, curly-haired, dark-skinned foreigner entering their building.

"Hello," Lucho said in his friendly Latin way. "I'm a Christian, a missionary. I live two blocks away."

"Are you living in the Missionary House?"

"Yes."

"Where are you from?"

"Colombia; but my wife and I work in Bolivia."

THE FARM AND THE SCHOOL

They welcomed Lucho and then invited him to pray with them but, unsure of this Latin fellow as they returned to their prayer time, some kept their eyes open while others prayed.

Although this assembly had helped provide the Missionary Home, the visiting missionaries inevitably bypassed them to go to bigger assemblies in the area. The brethren, surprised and happy that Lucho had come to visit, sent food baskets to their home and offered friendship and support in many ways.

During the fall, they asked Lucho to help them prepare a special program for Christmas. They planned to have an outreach to neighborhood families. Everything was ready. Lucho gave a Christmas message.

At the end, a brother, knowing Lucho had a good singing voice, said, "Lucho, how about leading us in some Christmas carols?"

Lucho looked aghast. He had never learned Christmas carols while growing up in Colombia. However, he was familiar with *Villancicos*, South American songs about the Nativity, with *burros* (donkeys), *vacas* (cows) and *ovejas* (sheep). Lucho recovered quickly. "I only know one Christmas carol in English. It is one that Lorna used to sing to our boys to amuse them on our many long trips by car: "Old MacDonald Had a Farm E-I-E-I-O."

He proceeded to divide the people into groups so that

GOD IS FAITHFUL

each could contribute an appropriate "Moo Moo," or "Baa Baa."

When Lucho got home that evening, Lorna asked, "How did it go?"

"Great! I gave the message and we sang the Christmas carol, 'Old MacDonald Had a Farm.'"

"What!" Lorna responded, "That's not a carol. It's not even a Christian song. I'm glad I wasn't there—I would have been totally embarrassed."

In spite of the unusual Christmas program, Lucho and Lorna developed a deep friendship with the Christians and the small assembly appreciated Lucho's help. About five months later, they left Scotland and returned to Bolivia. That was in 1982.

Thirteen years later, Lucho and Lorna were continuing their missionary work in Trinidad, Bolivia. They operated a "Children's Outreach Project" at the local chapel. Each day after school, they and fellow believers provided tutoring, help with homework, sports activities, a health program, food, and Bible devotions. Lucho wanted to upgrade this outreach to become a school, so they applied to the government for permission to start a Christian school. The government was not opposed to the idea of a school, but required more property for recreation. Lucho and the believers prayed that the Lord would provide more space.

THE FARM AND THE SCHOOL

A man and his wife owned an empty lot across the street from the chapel. The 3000-square-meter lot would be adequate for their needs.

A few months later, an unknown assailant shot and killed the man across the street. His wife recounted that before his death he had instructed her, "If ever we have to sell the property, let's give the people across the street the first chance to buy it." His widow carried out his wishes by offering to sell them the land for a fair market value, $40,000 US.

Lucho took this as a sign from the Lord. "Can you give us one year to get the $40,000?" She agreed. At the same time, they scraped together all the funds they could find for a deposit on the property—$5000.

They prayed all year, but only managed to save another $3000. The deadline loomed before them.

One day before it's completion, the lady across the street paid them a visit. "Are you ready to close the deal?"

"I'm sorry," Lucho responded, "we don't have the money."

"Well, I've already spent the $5000 deposit that you gave me a year ago. I cannot return it to you. I expect the remainder of the payment." The lady, an unbeliever, had attended the chapel occasionally and now reminded him of his own sermons: "I've heard you preach that if you believe in God, He will provide. I'll give you one more

GOD IS FAITHFUL

day. At your prayer meeting tonight, you be sure and ask God to provide the money!" she instructed.

Lucho's face became flushed as he listened to this unsolicited sermon from a non-believer. He wanted her to go away. Later, at prayer meeting he was still agitated. "Brethren, we must pray that the Lord will give us wisdom to convince this lady we cannot buy the lot." The Bolivian believers didn't pay any attention to Lucho and continued to pray that the Lord would provide the money in time.

The next morning, the Christians met at 7:00 AM to pray again. At 9:00 AM, the lady came across the street to see Lucho. "What's happening? Are you buying the property?" she inquired.

"Come back this afternoon," Lucho said, brushing her off.

At 10:00 AM, a Bolivian believer, administrator of the project, came running. "Lucho, a lady wants to talk to you on the phone."

"Who is it?"

"I don't know, but it's an overseas call and she speaks English."

Lucho went to the phone. "Hello. Who's calling?"

"It's Margaret."

"Hello, Margaret," he said, even though he couldn't identify exactly which Margaret he was speaking to.

THE FARM AND THE SCHOOL

"We have been praying for you and wondered if there was any special need you had at this time?"

Lucho knew that Assembly Christians in Britain didn't like anyone to talk about money! He couldn't be sure of her reaction, but decided to take the risk anyway and tell of their need since she had asked. "We need, right now, $40,000 US. Can you pray for that?"

"Do you have a bank account?" she responded.

"Yes."

"Do you know the number of your account?"

"Yes."

"I'll deposit the money for you right now!"

Lucho's heart raced as he hung up the phone. The Bolivian believers saw him run to his house to get Lorna. After telling her the news, he called them together. "I have important news."

"We know," one of them interrupted, "The Lord has provided the money."

Lorna decided to call Margaret for more details. "How did the Lord provide such a large sum of money on the very day we needed it?"

"Do you remember the little Gospel Hall in Newarthill?" Margaret asked. "One of the old men was my father. He never forgot Lucho's willingness to help. When the older believers died, they wanted the proceeds from the sale of the Hall to go to your ministry. Well, the building has been sold and all the paper work done; I called to carry out the wishes of the brethren who remembered your kindness to them."

Lucho and Lorna and the Bolivian believers praised God for providing for their needs. Now, Lucho sings a new version of his self-proclaimed Christmas carol.

Old MacDonald had a farm, and Lucho has a school....

Lucho's story reminds us of the promise found in Ecclesiastes 11:1, *"Cast thy bread upon the waters: for thou shalt find it after many days."*

THIRTY

God Chooses His Servants

James Lees, Scottish miner, took a return ticket to Sweden to test whether God would have him labor there in the gospel. He stayed to do a remarkable work in which hundreds of souls were saved. Pressing on throughout Europe, he visited Estonia, Poland, Austria, Yugoslavia, and the Balkans, preaching the gospel to thousands as well as delivering tons of food and clothing to the refugees of those lands during and after the Second War.

The Victorian era—mellow, peaceful, stately—was drawing towards its close with no premonition of danger and trouble ahead. Europe lay apparently at rest, its dynasties carelessly enjoying their ancient splendors, heedless of latent threats from Nihilism or popular upsurge. For a brief while yet its chancellories would congratulate themselves on the persistence of peace, and permit themselves prolonged holidays.

The most prescient of men could not foresee that Europe's dynasties were on the point of tottering to their fall, that few of its monarchs would retain their ancient thrones. But God knew, and God, who loves the poor empty rich, prepared His instrument to carry to them the news of His soul-satisfying love, which should radically change their own outlook and through them, that of ten thousand thousands beside.

LORD RADSTOCK

God chose for this errand an aristocrat, for He had to get the ear of emperors and kings. Unerringly He selected Lord Radstock, saved him by His grace through the testimony of a godly mother, and developed him in His own wonderful way.

By a series of what some would call curious coincidences, but which the Christian recognizes as the predetermined ordering of God, Lord Radstock found himself in Paris, with two princesses from Russia enquiring with hungry hearts for the satisfaction which is in Christ alone. Kneeling there they found Him to be as they expressed it, "My own Saviour for ever."

The newly-converted Grand Duchess invited Radstock to the capital, then called St. Petersburg, and a great wave of blessing flowed from his visit. God was not only intent on saving the aristocracy then present, but in preparing

GOD CHOOSES HIS SERVANTS

the way for subsequent servants of His. Many nobles and court officials were saved. Tens of thousands of New Testaments were distributed. Prayer meetings were commenced, to which the humbler folk gladly flocked.

On one of his return visits home, Lord Radstock asked a friend who was enquiring about the wonderful work then going on: "In what class of society, do you think is the largest percentage of truly converted people to be found?" The friend hazarded a guess: perhaps among the middle classes, or the working classes? Lord Radstock* replied: "I think not: I believe that the highest proportion is to be found among the crowned heads of Europe!"

---

* While it was common for many of Lord Radstock's landed gentry friends to relinquish their estates, auction off their china and silver, and give the proceeds to the work of the Lord, he did not sell everything. He kept his house in Mayfield Park. His biographer, Robert Fountain writes: "It meant employing ten servants and he kept beautiful china and silver; but he needed to do that in order to keep in contact with those of his own station in life…He invited such people to his home in order to witness to them." But he was very careful not to live selfishly. His housemaid remarked, "He sold paintings and horses in order to send money to relieve those who suffered from famine in India." And Fountain recounts, "On one occasion, going by train, when he was using third-class travel, someone asked him, 'Why do you travel third-class?' He said, 'Because there is no fourth-class.'"

THE DEVIL WON'T WIN

As in so many similar circumstances, God permitted the enemy of souls to hinder His work just when it seemed most promising. The aristocratic leaders of gospel revival were banished; less influential converts were sent to Siberia. It looked as though Satan had triumphed.

While Lord Radstock was quietly continuing his work on the basis of going wherever he was welcomed and preaching to rich and poor alike, in Sweden and Denmark, in Finland and among Russian emigrés in Paris, God was preparing another man to carry on His work.

FREDERICK W. BAEDEKER

The man whom God selected, prepared and sent forth was Dr. Baedeker, whose tireless journeys throughout Russia and Siberia are still fresh in the memory of older Christians. With an Imperial permit to freely use the Russian railways for his own travels and for the transport of Scriptures, and with permission to visit prisons with the gospel, the labors of this veteran make fascinating reading. He scattered the seed of the Word far and wide.

The Russian, ever more of an evangelist than a teacher, with a fanatical zeal born of repression, passed on the good news, and groups of believers came into being in many of the cities and towns of that vast country.

GOD CHOOSES HIS SERVANTS

E. H. BROADBENT

Meanwhile God was preparing yet another instrument for His work and, as the century had almost run out, He led E. Hamer Broadbent to Berlin. Equipping himself well with German there, and with French in Switzerland, Mr. Broadbent commenced a work of visitation of scattered believers for which he was eminently suited—a work which has had a profound effect on evangelical witness throughout north, central and southeast Europe.

Possessing the gift of the teacher, it was Mr. Broadbent's delight to seek out lonely believers, struggling assemblies, tried and persecuted Christians, and minister Christ to them. He was not a denominational sheep-stealer but a true shepherd, introducing these scattered sheep to the green pastures of the Word. Whether it were a Bible reading with a Greek Orthodox metropolitan or with naval officers of a foreign power, or with peasants in their hovels, farmers in the Crimea, students crowding in from the universities with their professors, the intelligentsia or the humble working people of European cities or Siberian plains, he was completely at home with them and they with him.

But even while he was in the heyday of his influence, God was quietly preparing an entirely different type of man for His work. In years to come the torch was to fall from Hamer Broadbent's hands, and many wondered whether its flame would be extinguished. But another runner was ready, another hand grasped the torch, held it aloft and carried it steadily forward. The hand was that of James Lees.

JAMES LEES

It was while Lord Radstock was busy sowing the seed of the gospel in Russia and neighboring countries that the Lord of the harvest made preparations for one to follow up his work. Yet knowing that by the time his successor was ready, revolutionary changes would have taken place in Europe, God passed by the dwellings of the well-to-do and stayed His footsteps by a working man's door.

So it was that on March 17, 1879, James Lees was born, the youngest in a family of five sons and three daughters. His father was a miner, working in Annbank, Ayrshire, Scotland. When James was three years old, the family moved to Burnbank. It is on record that at five years of age James often preached to his mother on Joseph and his brethren, and other Scripture subjects which appealed to his young mind. His mother encouraged him, "Go on, my son, you'll be a preacher yet!"

James Lees has left for us in his own words the story of his conversion, which took place on January 13, 1895.

Although scarcely sixteen years of age, I was acquainted with

GOD CHOOSES HIS SERVANTS

every theater, music hall and concert room in Glasgow, and my own native town. My ambition was to be an actor. I purposed joining the local Amateur Dramatic Club when I was sixteen. However, the greatest event in my life happened two months before, which gave me another ambition, namely, to please and serve Him who died on Calvary to make me His own.

On a Sunday evening toward the end of 1894, I found myself seated in a Gospel Hall, a very unusual place for me. God seemed to be in the place; the gospel was preached in power. Christ crucified was evidently set forth. The Spirit of God was speaking to me. Innumerable evils compassed me about; my iniquities took hold of me so that I could not look up. They were more than the hairs of my head. It was for the removal of all these sins that God's beloved Son left the glories of heaven, came to earth, and died.

On New Year's Day I attended two places of entertainment. In the evening I sat in the largest pantomime in Glasgow. The best artists in the country were on the stage. I must confess I did not seem to see them. God be praised, His Spirit had not ceased striving with me. All I seemed to see were the words, "Where will you be in eternity?" I left that large hall, anything but entertained.

A few nights later, passing along Quarry Street in Hamilton, a gospel tract was handed to me and an invitation given to attend a gospel meeting, which I accepted. Before retiring I read the tract. It did not take long. There were only a few words:

'If I die tonight, I will be in H—.'

What terse, naked truth! Yes, all will be in H—; black and

GOD IS FAITHFUL

white, red and yellow, rich and poor, educated and illiterate, will ultimately reach and be in eternity in Heaven or in Hell. Which? I dreaded to fill in the word. I could not write 'Heaven,' because I was not on the way to it. I dreaded to fill in 'Hell.'

Saturday evening found me in a concert hall. Among the artists were two comedians. They endeavored to entertain the crowd by singing a song to the tune of a well-known hymn. I felt it so irreverent I stood up on my seat in the gallery, looking down to the stage, feeling we were all fools and wondering if the greater fools were on the stage or in the gallery. I left the hall, saying, 'Goodbye; you'll see me no more.' What an empty heart! I had renounced the world, but this is not conversion. My heart was empty, for Christ was not there.

The following night I was seated with seven hundred hearers, listening to the gospel preached faithfully and clearly in Kensington Hall, Hamilton. I had decided not to leave till I could say, 'Jesus is mine!' The crowd left the hall but I remained. A Christian gentleman approached me with Bible in hand, and read several scriptures, I was not acquainted with in the Word. He read such glorious verses as John 3:16, John 5:24, and Romans 10:9. Looking up into the dear man's fact, I said, 'Sir, do you think if I accept the Lord Jesus He will accept me?'

'Of course He will!'

I believe he read John 6:37, *'Him that cometh to Me I will in no wise cast out.'* And I came; in other words, I accepted the Lord Jesus Christ as my own Saviour.

GOD CHOOSES HIS SERVANTS

About the year 1907, with the commendation of his brethren in Burnbank, he gave up his employment and stepped out in dependence on the Lord to devote all his time to the preaching of the gospel.

His first step was to join William Gray in pioneering in the needy county of East Lothian, moving around as they felt directed by the Spirit of God. Tent services were held at Tranent, Macmerry, North Berwick and Dunbar, though not without strong opposition from the enemy of souls through the bigotry and hostility of man.

Together these men labored untiringly in the gospel until Mr. Gray's death. Shortly after that, James Lees moved into the north of England, and southwards into Durham. When he was in West Hartlepool with Mr. Angus McKinnon working a tent, they met a Christian sailor from Sweden, who laid the need of his country on their hearts. Their interest thus awakened, Mr. McKinnon went over to Gothenburg in January 1910, and joined at once with the little assembly gathering in Skolgatan.

Fifteen years had passed since James Lees' conversion, fifteen years well-filled with the study of the Word to feed his own soul, and with the preaching of the same Word; output balancing intake. Unknown to himself, God had been preparing His servant for the task which He knew awaited him. They had been necessary years, for God's tools take time in forging, chilling, heating and tempering before they acquire a cutting edge that will last their allotted sphere of work. Fifteen years was none too long; but now God's clock had struck.

Looking to the Lord for guidance, James bought a two-week return ticket to Sweden—and forfeited the return half, for when he came to use it three years after, it had expired long since.

A NEW SPHERE OF LABOR

It was James Lees' intention to spend the two weeks looking around to discover for himself whether the Lord was indeed calling him to Sweden, or whether it was merely an idea of his own. So it was with a godly curiosity that he began to look around him and endeavor to gauge the real spiritual need of the Swedish people.

Sweden, as James Lees found it, was a fine nation with noble traditions and a proud history. Strongly Protestant, entrenched in centuries-old religious teaching, it hung tenaciously to the doctrine of baptismal regeneration and to the punctilious observance of the Church's rites. Like the Lutheran church in Germany and Protestant churches generally, it was indignant at the very thought that one might possess here and now eternal life and the assurance of sins forgiven. Of course there were notable exceptions to the general outlook and in due course these welcomed the newcomer.

GOD CHOOSES HIS SERVANTS

James Lees set himself to learn Swedish and made surprising strides in this none-too-easy language. He did not attempt to 'pick it up'—an attitude of mind for those easily satisfied that may merely mask mental laziness—but studied grammar in the hope of becoming proficient. That he succeeded is testified to by those qualified to judge; indeed, it was said of him in later years that he spoke Swedish as well as he spoke English.

In a very short time James was able to express himself in Swedish and even before he spoke it fluently he began to preach the simple gospel of the love and grace of God in the gift of His Son. Those who knew him in those days testify to his burning zeal in the gospel. His love for souls, so obvious in his preaching, caused the large crowds who came to hear him to forget any imperfections that there might be in the language. God honored His servant and many souls were saved, doors opening wide in every direction, and small companies in different places commencing to gather simply in the Lord's name. He was greatly loved, and although he denied himself the comforts of home-life—for he never married—the Lord gave him a home wherever he went.

On February 25, 1912, a great revival broke out which continued for a whole year and spread to many places in Sweden. As might it be expected, the enemy of souls reacted violently to this movement of the Spirit of God;

much opposition was stirred up, even by public authorities. There was much disturbance outside the halls, big stones were thrown through the windows, and it was not without risk to life and limb that the meetings could be maintained. James Lees was accused of being a "false teacher," and a "wolf in sheep's clothing," seeking to spread a false religion. But in spite of all the persecution hundreds were saved, young and old. As the fruits of this gracious revival were seen in the changed lives of many notorious sinners who had been saved, the opposition gradually died down. In one place the owner of a large estate, seeing the great change in the lives of many of his tenants and workpeople, gave sufficient materials for the erection of a building in which they could meet.

ESTONIA CALLING

Always pressing onward and looking to far horizons, James learned of the Protestant country of Estonia, on the eastern shore of the Baltic, whose people spoke or understood Swedish. Their knowledge of this language dated back to the early seventeenth century when the famous Swedish king, Gustavus Adolphus, took Estonia and other countries in his victorious advance. So, although their official and national tongue was Estonian—a difficult language, allied to Turkish and Finnish—their commercial language was Swedish. James Lees then found his parish enlarged by some two million souls, to whom he eagerly carried the message of life.

Arriving in the capital, Tallinn, he learned of the two islands of Dago and Wormso, a few miles westward, and these he visited with very great blessing. Indeed, it was said that thousands were converted. When the author met Mr. Lees in Tallinn in 1929, he learned that each year the assembly on one island would cross to the other to hold a conference and break bread together, alternating yearly. About a thousand believers thus kept alight annually the spirit of warm, brotherly love.

Three years had passed, years of ceaseless activity, of constant preaching and teaching, of *"journeyings oft,"* and James Lees returned home for a short while to report progress, and to give to his faithful band of earnest prayer-partners information to enable them to bear him up still more intelligently before God.

The upheaval of World War I did not hinder him; he was able to spend the time consolidating the work in Scandinavia, chiefly in Sweden. J. J. Adam joined him for a time as a beloved fellow-worker and, as soon as the war was over, they visited Finland and Estonia together.

MORE WORK TO DO

Ever his field was widening and now fresh countries beckoned him. It is a matter for thankfulness, in a brief

GOD IS FAITHFUL

lull of work during 1949, that Mr. Lees should have jotted down some rough notes of his journeyings, certainly never intended for publication, nor fit for it without careful revision. They follow here, and may be regarded as his own work, altered as little as possible.

The map of Europe changed considerably after the First World War. The breakup of Czarist Russia resulted in the formation of several new countries; Finland became more free than formerly; Poland was declared a republic; and the Baltic States—Estonia, Latvia, and Lithuania—came into being. The Austro-Hungarian Empire collapsed; Romania was enlarged, and large countries like Czechoslovakia and Yugoslavia, each with nearly 1.5 million people, were formed.

It may have been through contact with that wonderful man of God, Mr. E. H. Broadbent, missionary and traveller, author of *The Pilgrim Church,* that I became interested in Poland, and from Estonia I paid a visit to that country in 1925. When I arrived in the capital, Warsaw, I was most heartily received into the home of Mr. S. Zebrowski, who was formerly a Roman Catholic priest. He must have been very enthusiastic in that religion, for he collected sufficient money to build three R. C. churches in Warsaw and elsewhere, all three of which I visited.

He had a most wonderful conversion. To penitents at the confessional he used to say, *"Absolvo te,"* but he felt he needed his own sins forgiven. Taking a long vacation, he visited Palestine and

GOD CHOOSES HIS SERVANTS

Jerusalem, thinking he might find forgiveness at the grave of Jesus. He was soon to realize that this is only found through the living Saviour. He toured the United States seeking salvation but could not find it.

Back in his own country, he happened to hear of two nuns in Wilno, Poland's sixth largest city, who were speaking of salvation. When in their nunnery they had received a Bible, and through reading it had been led to Christ. Zebrowski visited these sisters in Christ and they led him to the Saviour.

He hurried back to his church in Warsaw to proclaim the simple gospel. Many believed, but many rejected his testimony. There was great commotion throughout the country, which compelled him to leave the Roman Catholic church, and those who had been saved left with him. They gathered in simple fashion around the Word of God.

At that time Poland was under Russia. A Russian Commissar asked him the name of his sect (all outside the R. C. Church are usually termed sectaries). He replied: "We have no name but Christians."

"We are all Christians," said the Commissar, "except the Jews."

"We are followers of the first Christians," said Zebrowski.

"That's a good name!" said the Commissar. So that group, and all similar groups were registered officially as "Followers of the First Christians." Like the Commissar, I, too, thought it a good name, and bless God for the many times I have been with these dear "followers of the first Christians" who followed Christ.

GOD IS FAITHFUL

Zebrowski was living in a summer villa eighteen kilometers out of Warsaw, as it was summertime. I shall never forget the first Lord's Day there when with German-speaking colonists and pure Poles we gathered around the Lord's Supper in the open air. A well-known English brother, Mr. Sydney R. Hopkins, a schoolmaster from Norwich, was present on holiday, and spoke on a few verses, *"Jesus Himself drew near"* (Lk. 24); *"Jesus Himself stood in the midst"* (Lk. 24:36); Jesus *"Himself shall descend"* (1 Thess. 4), etc., and surely Jesus Himself was with us that day. Mr. Hopkins went to another part and I went to the Polish Ukraine. We met again a month afterwards and were deeply impressed with the possibilities of the new Poland and the work of God in it.

Before leaving for the Ukraine, I made the acquaintance of an ex-priest named Przeorski who had lived for many years in Chicago where he became a priest in the Polish Catholic National Church. He returned to Poland where he met Zebrowski, who gave him a New Testament.

In his hotel room he read through the Gospel by John and, when the came to the fifteenth chapter, he was illuminated through the first five verses. He trusted in Christ, and told Zebrowski the next day that he had never had such a night in his life. What had happened? He knew nothing of conversion or regeneration but God had taught him. He was baptized three days later, and became a real Bible teacher.

I can never forget my first visit to Polish Ukraine with its millions of Ukrainians among whom God had been at work. Before

GOD CHOOSES HIS SERVANTS

the Second World War there were at least 25,000 decided Christians. I met there two English couples, not associated with any missionary association, doing a magnificent work along the Polish Ukraine—Mr. and Mrs. David Griffiths, and Mr. and Mrs. Stuart Hine. Them I found to be Christians with a hold on God. Meetings in all places visited were large, long, and good, and souls were saved.

A well-known Hebrew Christian, superintendent of a Bible School for Russians in the US, pressed me to go with them to a large village and he would interpret for me. Our only means of travel proved to be the long, four-wheeled farm-cart with open sides. What a ride! and what roads! When half-way there I asked, "Are there any Christians near here where I can stay and await your return? I am afraid if I advance further in this cart all my theology will be shaken out of me!"

I took part in a large conference; German colonists and Poles came long distances, and God's presence was in those gatherings. Mr. Goetze interpreted for me. A colporteur accompanied me in the train to the conference, and it was interesting to watch how he secured an ear for the reading of the Scriptures. When the train stopped at a station the guard performed his duty as quickly as possible and was back again in our large open carriage to listen.

On returning to Warsaw, Zebrowski said to me, "Something wonderful has happened since you were here. There is a Government official and God is dealing with him. He is in soul-trouble, and his wife said he was ill but he assured her he was not physi-

GOD IS FAITHFUL

cally ill, it was soul-sickness. 'I am wondering where I shall spend eternity' he said. He maintained and many times he has told me the same that it was as if a voice within him said, 'Telephone 6002 and someone will tell you how you can find peace.' The intelligent, educated Pole thought it foolish to do so but this voice continued for three days. He took up the telephone and called the number 6002 which proved to be that of Mr. Zebrowski. The latter was now a Director in an insurance firm.

Krakiewicz, the government official in question, told his story and Zebrowski asked him over to his office. They read Acts 10 together about Cornelius and Peter. Zebrowski asked if he would come to a meeting on the Sunday evening when he would he interpreting for an Englishman. He brought his wife, and also on the following evening. Souls were being saved.

At the end of a meeting, while we were all standing, someone at the back prayed. I asked Zebrowski what he said? The answer was, "It is Krakiewicz: he is thanking God for salvation." That was a full surrender. If Krakiewicz got Christ that night, Christ got all there was of Krakiewiez.

God does not deal with souls in London like this, but in dark Warsaw, where there is little gospel light, God will give telephone numbers.

Ransome W. Cooper, *James Lees: Shepherd of the Lonely Sheep in Europe,* London: Pickering & Inglis, pp. 11-18, 22-33